GOD'S GIFT OF SCIENCE

GOD'S GIFT
of SCIENCE

Theological Presuppositions Underlying
Exploration of the Natural World

GRAEME FINLAY

CASCADE *Books* · Eugene, Oregon

GOD'S GIFT OF SCIENCE
Theological Presuppositions Underlying Exploration of the Natural World

Cascade Books
An Imprint of Wipf and Stock Publishers
199 W. 8th Ave., Suite 3
Eugene, OR 97401

www.wipfandstock.com

PAPERBACK ISBN: 978-1-6667-4806-2
HARDCOVER ISBN: 978-1-6667-4807-9
EBOOK ISBN: 978-1-6667-4808-6

Cataloguing-in-Publication data:

Names: Finlay, Graeme, 1953– [author]
Title: God's gift of science : theological presuppositions underlying exploration of the natural world / Graeme Finlay.
Description: Eugene, OR: Cascade Books, 2022 | Includes bibliographical references and index.
Identifiers: ISBN 978-1-6667-4806-2 (paperback) | ISBN 978-1-6667-4807-9 (hardcover) | ISBN 978-1-6667-4808-6 (ebook)
Subjects: LCSH: Religion and science | Science—Philosophy | Human ecology—Religious aspects—Christianity | Nature—Religious aspects—Christianity
Classification: BL240.2 F56 2022 (paperback) | BL240.2 (ebook)

VERSION NUMBER 101822

"May we see, know, and understand the wonder of God's creation, and from that understanding, both from our science and our theology, act upon it to be better stewards of creation."
Sir Ghillian Prance, *The Earth under Threat*, 25

"It is vital, not only for nature, but for the future health of the church itself, that we have a well-developed theology of creation and of Christian stewardship. If there is to be any hope . . . then the church must give a lead because it has so much to offer in its rich theology of creation and stewardship."
Sir Ghillian Prance, *The Earth under Threat*, 66

CONTENTS

LIST OF FIGURES AND TABLES

ACKNOWLEDGEMENTS

I AM DEEPLY GRATEFUL to the editorial and production staff of Wipf and Stock for their courtesy, efficiency, and professional rigor. In particular, my editor Revd Dr Robin Parry has been invariably patient, helpful, and insightful—at all times a pleasure to work with.

INTRODUCTION

CERTAIN PEOPLE WITH A militant atheist perspective have asked the question as to whether theology has ever contributed to human knowledge or well-being. Such people ask this question rhetorically, fully expecting the answer to be "No." Their style of bravado is intimidating, but it is evidence that they are ignorant of, and even disdain, the lessons of history.

Christian theology informed and inspired the development of many thoroughly humane aspects of the societies in which it has been pursued. It has pioneered ideas of human equality and rights, has led the charge against slavery, and underlies the democratic vision. It has generated motivations for the care of people who are poor and unwell—who suffer both physically and mentally—and who are vulnerable to exploitation or neglect. Ancient historian Edwin Judge has said that the social and personal values most sought after by secular liberal people originated not from Athens but from Jerusalem—not from Greek philosophy or precedent but from the Judeo-Christian tradition.[1] Theologian Theo Hobson has said that "Secular humanism, despite being secular, is firmly rooted in Christianity. Its moral universalism is an adaptation, or mutation, of Christianity."[2] We forget to our peril the benefits of the Christian revolution.[3]

We live in an age of rampant misinformation (unsubstantiated rumor) and disinformation (frank duplicity). Some people, hankering for a rock upon which the concept of truth may be defended, look to science. Surely (they think) its evidence-based mode of operation provides a final redoubt against the flood of falsehood, which threatens to sweep away all before it. But the sources underpinning chapter 1 of this book demonstrate that

1. Judge, "Religion," 307–19.
2. Hobson, God Created, 3–4.
3. Hart, Atheist Delusions; Spencer, Evolution; Holland, Dominion.

science is not a free-standing exercise. Science is at its most healthy when it is pursued in a suitable nurturing moral or spiritual environment. We should expect that the development of science would be facilitated by a worldview that celebrates the cosmos as being objectively real, intelligible, consistent in its operations, and even good—that is, worthy of study. The rise of science had to be contingent upon a prior metaphysical truthfulness.

We proceed to consider the character and source of this appropriate nurturing *milieu*. Chapters 2 and 3 describe how the character of God, as revealed in the Hebrew and Christian scriptures, provided the metaphysical bedrock on which the scientific enterprise has been able to operate.

At this point, we can anticipate the argument by considering proposals from two erudite and highly acclaimed scholars who have investigated the origins of science.

The historian John Hedley Brooke, in his 1991 classic, *Science and Religion*, set out four models that seek to describe the relationships between what he called "religion" and science. *Religion* refers here to Christianity as it developed in the West, but it is a vague term that may be confounded by narrow factionalism, political loyalties, or purely selfish egos.[4]

The first option is a *conflict* model—that religion and science have always been in opposition. The media often feature a conflict (or warfare) model because it makes for racy stories. Despite its popularity, and aggressive promotion by the ageing New Atheists, the conflict model is rejected by historians of science as being vacuous. It turns out that Darwin's bulldog, T. H. Huxley, promulgated the conflict idea for "political" purposes: because the church had always sponsored science and Huxley wanted to make more space for secular professionals. His aim was understandable, but by demonizing the church he inverted the truth to achieve his aim.

A second option is for a *complementary* relationship. Religion and science ask different questions, use different methodologies, and involve different domains of experience. Therefore, some people conclude, these fields of thought do not interact with each other. They are non-overlapping. But this idea has major flaws. In practice, people cannot keep the subjects separate. Those most vociferous about the supremacy of science cannot resist pronouncing on God, purpose, values, and ethics, and they dress some branches of science in an atheistic metaphysical garb. Other people, by contrast, find that science points beyond itself.[5] It invites questions about

4. Brooke, *Science and Religion*, 2–5.
5. Polkinghorne, *One World*, 63.

the mystery of being—the wonder that there is a mathematically ordered, anthropic cosmos—and the nature of personality, beauty, love, and justice. In any case, theology and the historical sciences (cosmology, biological evolution) do in fact use similar approaches.[6]

The third model is that of *cooperation*. Scholars have argued that scientific activity requires assumptions about the nature of the world that reflect religious beliefs. Scientific pioneers of the seventeenth century (Galileo, for example) were greatly indebted to ideas developed by Catholic theologians of the medieval period. Puritan values further facilitated the development of science in the seventeenth century. Much evidence supports this model, but it is clouded by those occasions when Christian people have not accepted the findings of science (for diverse reasons, not necessarily *theological* ones).

Brooke himself prefers the model of *complexity*. There is "an extraordinarily rich and complex" interaction between religion and science[7] (which, for much of its development, was known by the much more inclusive term *natural philosophy*). It follows that every episode of engagement between "religion" (in whatever form that may be) and science requires close examination in its own right.

An alternative approach is to ask, more specifically, how biblical theology has affected the development of the scientific mindset. The astrophysicist-theologian Christopher Kaiser, in another 1991 classic, *Creation and the History of Science*, focused on the influence of the theological tradition that saw the cosmos as being "subject to a single code of law that was established along with the universe at the beginning of time."[8] God had ordained such lawful behavior, within the limits of which nature would operate freely.

Brooke suggests that theological ideas have provided the presuppositions of the scientific enterprise by underwriting the uniformity of the relations between cause and effect.[9] First, the biblical concept of creation presupposed an intelligent divine law-giver who ordained laws in nature. It also implied that the created human mind was "matched to the intelligibility of nature" and was capable of understanding its ordered processes. Second, religion provided justification for science in an age when experimental work was deemed to be useless or even plain ridiculous. The thesis that

6. Polkinghorne, *Reason and Reality*, 15.

7. Brooke, *Science and Religion*, 6–7.

8. Kaiser, *Creation and the History of Science*, 6.

9. Brooke, *Science and Religion*, 19–26.

religion gave sanction to a nascent science (widely lampooned for its work on the weight of air, or the anatomy of fleas, for example) has been strongly advocated by Peter Harrison.[10] Third, religious motivations for developing science included the hope of improving the lot of humanity. Fourth, the idea that God was freely active in nature engendered a new spirit of empiricism. One had to look at nature to see what God had done. Writing and reading commentaries on ancient texts was no longer sufficient for engaging with nature. A more observant scientific methodology was fostered as a result of these attitudes.

Kaiser also saw four main effects of the tradition that recognized God as creator.[11] First, it nurtured the expectation that the world was comprehensible. Second, heaven and earth could be recognized as parts of the one integrated reality, so repudiating the idea that the stars were supernatural beings. Third, God ordained and guaranteed the lawfulness of nature, within the bounds of which the creatures could operate autonomously. "The autonomy of nature is thus 'relative' in the sense of being relational (to God) as well as in the sense of not being self-originated or entirely self-determined."[12] And fourth, there was the practical consideration that the church was called to the service of healing and restoration. Compassion that was manifested in practical care led to developments in anatomy, surgery, and therapeutics. In other words, concern for those suffering the effects of disease facilitated the study of the form and function of the human body.

These potted summaries will be elaborated in chapters 2 and 3 of this book. Suffice it to say here that the biblical, Hebraic worldview affected the ontology, epistemology and cosmology of Europe at the deepest level during the time when science arose as a self-perpetuating enterprise.[13] Science was gestated in the womb of biblical theology. The converse of this hypothesis of scientific origins is the question of what might happen to an established scientific program if it becomes starved of those supportive biblical foundations. This will be discussed in chapter 4.

Christian theological insights, like the findings of science, are often surprising, as discussed in chapter 5. The element of surprise, of being arrested or even shocked by new information, is significant. It implies that we are engaging with a reality that is independent of us. We have not

10. Harrison, "Religion," 255–71.

11. Kaiser, *Creation and the History of Science*, 7–51

12. Kaiser, *Creation and the History of Science*, 15.

13. Turner, "Recasting," 166.

constructed it. We do not make God in our image, nor are electrons mere fictions invented by middle-class males. This common feature of theology and science contributes to the satisfaction of their pursuit and to our confidence in the independence of our subject-matter and the validity of our findings.

Finally, when the findings of science impact human lives, their application still needs theological input. Scientific developments should be subjected to theological assessments before they are applied to human living. If we are able to achieve some techno-scientific feat, it does not follow that we should release it widely in society. At the time of writing, the metaverse of virtual reality is awaited keenly, but how might the widespread availability of this technical wizardry affect human health, relationality, or groundedness in the real world? J. R. Oppenheimer, who led the project to develop the atomic bomb, stated that when something "is technically sweet, you go ahead and do it." However, after the bomb was detonated, he said he had known sin.[14] If only theological scrutiny had been brought to bear on the atomic bomb project at an earlier stage!

The concluding chapter considers an urgent challenge in which theology and science provide mutual illumination: the way humans exploit the biosphere, and the resulting human-induced ecological damage. There are many wonderful, devoted people (Greenpeace, Avaaz) living sacrificially and passionately to turn humanity back from its mindless rush to ecological destruction. There are also many sincere Christians (especially in high-income countries and in cities) who are uninterested in ecological sustainability and the effects of their traditional lifestyles on people in low-income countries who are vulnerable to desertification, flooding, and encroaching seas.

To both groups of people, I believe that a vital element should be added to their mindsets. Humanity should heed God's call to a changed heart and vision, to the kingdom of God, to cherish the promise of *shalom*, God's wholeness, in the world. Chapter 6 represents a dialogue between erudite and perceptive scholars: the secular ecological economist Bill Rees, and the ecologically concerned theologian Michael Northcott,[15] supplemented by Lawrence Osborn, Richard Bauckham, Kevin Durrant, and the theologian-scientist combo of Spencer and White.

14. Gingerich, *God's Universe*, 109.

15. Northcott, *Moral Climate*; and his articles "Ecology and Christian Ethics," 209–27; "Spirit," 167–74; "Sustaining Ethical Life," 225–40.

I first came across Bill Rees's writings in a 2003 essay in *Nature* entitled "A Blot on the Land." His work is a lucid and illuminating description of the ecological crisis and its connections with human activities. With his former student Mathis Wackernagel, Rees created the concept of the *ecological footprint* as well as derivative ideas (the number of earths our lifestyle requires; and *overshoot day*, that ever-earlier point in the year by which humanity has used up its annual allocation of resources). Rees provides insightful and rather despondent analyses of human nature and its seeming inability to countenance reality and respond morally.

Our analysis of the destruction of planet earth must go further. Biblical theology provides elements required for an adequate response to the destruction of the ecosphere: the justice of God, which is inscribed deeply into the structure of the physical and biological creation; concepts of sin and repentance; the prophetic foundations of democracy, whether political or economic; and the abiding hope that God's purposes for a transformed creation will be realized.

Faith in a creator God provides a basis for response. The energy must come from passion: wonder and delight in our encounter with creation, grief over our sin, love for God and his world, worship and amazement at the redemption achieved by Jesus the Messiah and the ever-working Spirit of God.

> Our Lord and God! You are worthy
> to receive glory, honor, and power.
> For you created all things,
> and by your will they were given existence and life.[16]

This book summarizes my reflections over a working lifetime. I have cited scholars who wrote forty years ago (or more) who have had a formative influence on my understanding. There are dangers here. One danger is that their ideas have been superseded by more recent scholarship. I hope that I have been alert to that. There has been no past golden age. But perhaps the greater danger is that wisdom of past generations has been forgotten, displaced by fashionable mores, or buried under the flow of trivia by which our minds are assailed.

I write as a Christian who, for his working life, has been immersed in cancer research and the teaching of scientific pathology. I have been exposed to incessant dialogue and debate of varying tone pertaining to

16. Rev 4:11.

the theology-science interface. Some of the issues on which I write have become politicized. People might wonder whether I promote perspectives of the "Left" or of the "Right". My deep hope is that my thoughts are not formed by such ideologies, but that they reflect biblical faith, which transcends contemporary polarities. (It has been pointed out that each of certain positions over which society is currently polarized has been selectively borrowed from biblical traditions.)[17] I have found difficulty in writing on certain subjects (especially that of chapter 6 pertaining to just and sustainable living), because I am deeply aware of my inability to live up to the ethical implications of the scientific, moral, and spiritual analyses described.

I have used footnotes liberally—I am not a historian or an economist or an ecologist. I feel that I must acknowledge with care the erudite sources from which I have gleaned my information. Some of the contents of this book were explored in preliminary form elsewhere. In particular, I have reflected briefly on the role of biblical faith in providing the worldview in which science could flourish,[18] and on moral challenges arising from ecological-footprint analysis.[19]

17. Spencer, *Evolution*, 38, 185; Holland, *Dominion*, 533.

18. Finlay, *Gospel*, 23–45.

19. Finlay, *Gospel*, 194–204.

1

SCIENCE IS NOT SELF-SUFFICIENT

WE LIVE IN AN age of so-called alternative facts. Pressure groups concoct controversies ("is smoking *really* bad for your health?") and demand platforms to promote their own points of view. Wild conspiracy theories spread rapidly and widely. Politicians and other celebrities who peddle gross falsehoods carry credulous supporters along with them. Commentators fret over who, if anyone, should control the content of social media. We seem to be heading towards life in a moral vacuum.

In response to this deepening ethical crisis, we have been advised to put our hope in science as the bedrock of truth.[1] We are faced with "truth decay" and are told that it is the evidence-based thinking of science that is the only foundation upon which we can address the desperate plight in which democracy finds itself.[2]

What is this thing called *science*? Natural science is the quest to understand the structure of the physical world and the processes that occur in it. Its scope covers entities that range in size from the subatomic world of quantum physics to cosmology, and from the molecules of life to ecological relations in the biosphere. Science seeks to make careful observations of phenomena and formulate hypotheses (that is, to generate ideas) that might explain the mechanisms underlying those processes. Hypotheses include predictions of how matter should behave under particular conditions. These predictions are tested by experiments, the results of which are

1. Nola, "Courage Needed."
2. Holt, "Democracy's Plight," 433.

8

interpreted to support, modify, or discard hypotheses.[3] The generation and testing of hypothesis constitute an ongoing cycle of investigation.

Natural science has been amazingly successful in elucidating the workings of matter, including the operation of matter in living organisms. Science and scientists have gained a high degree of prestige. Science is indeed an amazing cultural achievement. But this prestige has arisen because of the modesty of scientific ambitions.[4] To do science requires a self-limitation on the part of scientists. As they prepare to ply their trade, they make a prior commitment that they will investigate *only* the interactions of matter and energy in time and space. Scientists recognize that their measuring devices—such as thermometers, microscopes, spectroscopes—enable them to probe only material reality. It is this narrow focus that has given science such power.

In order to embark on their work, scientists thus deliberately avoid the gamut of considerations pertaining to themselves as *persons*. They exclude work on ethics (love, justice, and compassion) and aesthetics (music, poetry, and art), purpose and meaning, and religious, ideological, and political beliefs.[5] The key point is that science *does not* and *cannot* deny the reality or importance of ethics, aesthetics, purpose, and the rest of our worldview components. Science must ignore them *in principle* because it does not possess the tools to tease them apart.[6] This necessary limitation

3. Some areas of science do not lend themselves to experiments. Historical sciences such as astronomy, geology, evolutionary biology, and archaeology are *observational* sciences that progress by ever more detailed data collection and analysis. Even here, as Polkinghorne observed, "historical sciences, such as physical cosmology or evolutionary biology, rely for much of their explanatory power on the insights of the directly experimental sciences, such as physics and genetics." Polkinghorne, "Science and Religion Debate," 3.

4. Polkinghorne, "Science and Religion Debate," 6.

5. A gray area is psychology and sociology, in which persons investigate the nature of persons. Is mind capable of describing mind? The ways around this enigma are to objectivize persons or to use qualitative, descriptive ways of investigating mental realities. Donald MacKay stated that "students of human nature and human society . . . would like to be called 'scientists'; but in their particular line of investigation there is an epistemological snag. . . . They are people investigating *people*. Their own values and presuppositions . . . inevitably color not only what strikes them as worthy of investigation in the human situation facing them, but also what they perceive in it." MacKay suggested that this explains why some social scientists reject *all* objective science as a myth. Mackay, "Objectivity," 20–21.

6. It follows that when authors such as Peter Atkins or Richard Dawkins claim that science rules out the ontological reality of personal, ethical, or spiritual aspects of our

implies that there are ways of knowing *in addition to* the scientific one, and other categories of truth with which we may engage.

There is a problem with the sort of talk that describes science as being the "bedrock of truth." Science *cannot* be the "bedrock of truth" because science itself is dependent on a foundational, supportive worldview. Science cannot provide its own justification. As philosopher Roger Trigg has stated, "Those who say that science can answer all questions are themselves standing outside science to make that claim."[7] To stand "outside science" is to take a metaphysical (or religious) position. It follows that "there has to be a metaphysical framework in which science can be seen to operate."[8] Trigg has said that: "Science cannot escape philosophical assumptions about the framework in which its own activity takes place."[9] Science operates on underlying assumptions about the nature of reality. Consequently, the scientific enterprise is not a free-standing, autonomous human enterprise but requires prior beliefs that provide support for its activities.

Wagner and Briggs have stated that "the penultimate curiosity of science has throughout human history swum in the slipstream of an ultimate metaphysical curiosity."[10] In other words, through history, human reflection on the divine and on our nature as thinking beings (our primary interest) has promoted reflection on the physical world (our secondary interest). The link between contemplation of God and a desire to comprehend creation is rooted, as these authors go on to say, "in the human need to make sense of the world as a whole."

It is naive to assert an *either/or* choice between science and metaphysics. Rather, the connection is a *both/and* relationship in which the capacity to do science is based on a supportive worldview (Fig. 1). Oxford physics professor Andrew Steane has said "The relationship between faith and the scientific method is not one of logical alternatives, but one in which the latter is part of the former."[11] Thus Steane rejects the idea of two separate circles, one labelled "faith," and other "science." Instead, he places the

---

lives, they have forgotten the rules under which they entered science in the first place. If you choose to play tennis, you can't complain that there are no shuttlecocks.

7. Trigg, *Beyond Matter*, 54; or as Trigg states elsewhere, "Science cannot explain everything, and certainly not the preconditions of its own existence," ibid., 97.

8. Trigg, *Beyond Matter*, 143.

9. Trigg, "Does Science Need Religion?" 20.

10. Wagner and Briggs, *Penultimate Curiosity*, 411.

11. Steane, *Faithful to Science*, 36.

"science" circle entirely within the "faith" circle. Science is not the "bedrock of truth" but is an enterprise that rests upon some underlying foundation that sustains its activity.

People who assert that science is independent of metaphysical or "religious" considerations tend to be materialists (where materialism is itself a metaphysical stance, it should be noted). But as the nineteenth-century atheist Friedrich Nietzsche stated, "Strictly speaking, there is no such thing as science 'without any presuppositions' . . . a philosophy, a 'faith,' must always be there first, so that science can acquire from it a direction, a meaning, a limit, a method, a right to exist. . . . It is still a *metaphysical faith* that underlies our faith in science."[12] If we are to live truthfully, we should seek to discover the worldview that sustains and informs the scientific enterprise.

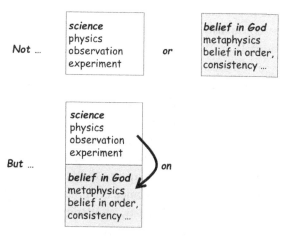

Fig. 1. Physics and/or metaphysics
Physics is not an alternative to metaphysics (or "religion"—a word subject to many different meanings) but is *built upon* an appropriately supportive worldview or belief system.

HOW INDEPENDENT IS SCIENCE?

There have been many attempts to argue that science is the only way of knowing, the sole route to encountering truth. Such projects invariably collapse into foolishness. For there is no way that science can demonstrate that

12. Quoted by Woods, *How the Catholic Church*, 81. Italics in original.

science is the only way to discovering truth. Science cannot demonstrate that there are no realities beyond those which lie within its rightful purview.

Skeptics have tried over recent centuries to dismiss religion. For instance, David Hume, an influential skeptic of the eighteenth century, criticized and rejected Christian faith. He wrote that if we read a work of theological literature, we should ask only two questions: "Does it contain any abstract reasoning concerning quantity or number?" and "Does it contain any experimental reasoning concerning matters of fact and existence?" Hume believed that the answer to these questions was "No," and that we should therefore commit any such theological work "to the flames. For it can contain nothing but sophistry and illusion."[13] The problem for Hume is that his own bold statement contained neither mathematical reasoning nor experimental data and so—*by his own two criteria*—should be burnt as worthless. Hume's statement, refuting metaphysics, was inherently metaphysical. Extraordinarily, the agnostic T. H. Huxley propounded the same fallacy a century later.[14]

In the early 1900s, a group called the Vienna Circle promoted the idea that a statement can be considered as possessing *meaning* only if it can be verified by science, and as possessing *truth* only if it is so verified. (In the English-speaking world, the philosopher A. J. Ayer promoted this idea as *logical positivism*.) This philosophy proposed that any claim to truth that could not be scientifically verified was metaphysical in nature and was therefore mere *nonsense*.[15] Such a claim, positivists said, did not even rise to the level of a truth claim, so it was denied even the dignity of being false. It was, according to the logical positivists, an utterance *without any meaning at all*. But this central tenet of logical positivism could not itself be verified by science. Presumably, this reduces the creed of logical positivism itself to the status of nonsense.[16] Logical positivism is now wholly discredited.

13. Quoted by Wagner and Briggs, *Penultimate Curiosity*, 414, 418.

14. Holland, *Dominion*, 445. Huxley said: "In matters of the intellect, do not pretend that conclusions are certain which are not demonstrated or demonstrable." This pronouncement is not empirically demonstrable. He thought that science was "the only method by which truth could be ascertained"—but this claim itself is not amenable to ascertainment by scientific methodology.

15. Trigg, *Beyond Matter*, 6–10, 55.

16. As indicated by Otto Neurath, who wrote in an article entitled "The Philosophy of the Vienna Circle" that philosophy was obsolete. See Trigg, *Beyond Matter*, 22–23.

Indeed, Ayer himself later confessed that the main problem with his book *Language, Truth, and Logic* is that "nearly all of it was false."[17]

The system of ideas known as *scientism* posits that only realities open to scientific investigation are real. A *scientistic* view of the mind sees all our reasoning as being equated with chains of neurochemical events in the brain. However, Trigg objects, if true this would mean "that independent rational judgment is impossible."[18] The logical connections between elements in a chain of reasoning are of a very different order to the physical connections between chains of electro-chemical events in the brain. The link between true premises and a conclusion, for instance, is not the kind of efficient causal link one finds between a physical cause and effect. If the former are reduced to the latter, then logic and reason lose their trustworthiness. Therefore, if scientism is true, we can have no confidence in the rational basis of scientism. As John Polkinghorne has said, "Thought is replaced by electro-chemical neural events."[19] If people reduce rationality and ideas about truth to only blips in the neural network of the brain, then "rational discourse dissolves into the absurd chatter of firing synapses."[20] We must give a place to rationality, wisdom, truth, and goodness as realities that are independent of us, and that our brains, in sustaining mind, allow us to access.

Sociobiologists argue that our genes control our beliefs and behaviors. If this is so, there is no reason by which we should respect the (genetically determined) beliefs and pronouncements of sociobiologists—for how can we know that their genes produce thoughts that are *true*?[21] As Polkinghorne has said, if the sociobiologists are to maintain their position, they "must grant *themselves* a tacit saving clause." That is, sociobiologists must assert that *only* sociobiologists are able to think in a way that is free from the domination of genes. "Otherwise, their conclusions are as much explained away in a purely reductive manner as would be the other aspects of human knowledge that they seek to subvert."[22] The sociobiologist may allow that there is a long leash between genes and behavior. Fair enough. But in that case the leash is clearly long enough to allow for genuine

17. Wagner and Briggs, *Penultimate Curiosity*, 418.
18. Trigg, *Beyond Matter*, 132.
19. Polkinghorne, *One World*, 92.
20. Polkinghorne, *One World*, 93.
21. Trigg, *Beyond Matter*, 108–10.
22. Polkinghorne, *Beyond Science*, 111.

creativity, rational investigation, moral responsibility, and authentic dynamic relationality with other personal beings. And once that is admitted sociobiological determinism has been abandoned and the door to independent agency characterized by a measure of free will is opened once again.

Freud proposed that our thought arises from unconscious sexual motivations and so is to be treated with suspicion (with the implication that if his thoughts on this matter are true, he must be an exception). Marx (or his disciples) posited that our thought comes from class and economic determinants (although to command our assent, his thought alone must have transcended the class and economic conditions in which he was raised).[23] Postmodernists write that texts have no particular meaning (their own texts excepted). Or they argue that "truth is a mere rhetorical device, employed in the service of oppression." If this is so their own claims are included and we should rightly ignore their rhetoric and oppressive intentions.[24] Each such form of "reductionist criticism" is *self-defeating* because it requires an "escape clause" exclusive to itself.[25] In the same way, all claims asserting the hegemony of scientific thought are in fact metaphysical. Science cannot justify its own existence.

The pursuit of science is an activity of human persons. As such, we would expect it to be promoted (or hindered) by aspects of our personal makeup—our outlook on reality. But where might we find a science-*sustaining* outlook? Here we come to the thesis of this book. It has been argued widely by historians that, during the gestation of science to the seventeenth century, *the God revealed in the histories of ancient Israel and of Jesus was the guarantor of the truth upon which science was (and still is) founded.* God is good and God's world is good, so finding out about the world (science) must be good.

Not everyone, of course, will concede that science is good. The nineteenth-century atheist Nietzsche "thought that scientific understanding is not intrinsically good. He thought that the belief that it is inherently good is an inheritance of the Christian tradition, and one that should be rejected

---

23. Marx may have allowed the "independent role of non-material creativity in social development"; it may have been his disciples who crudely posited that "sciences are deterministically produced from purely material causes." See Goodman and Russell, *Rise of Scientific Europe*, 3.

24. Wright, *New Testament and the People of God*, 61n35.

25. Polkinghorne, *Reason and Reality*, 7.

along with Christianity."[26] Nietzsche had the acumen to see that science was sustained by Christian faith. He would happily have rejected both.

Charles Coulson was a leading mid-twentieth-century physicist who made significant advances in chemical bond theory. He stated that "science is only possible in a community where certain religious beliefs are widely held." In support of this claim, he cited Archbishop Temple, who said that science "can never spontaneously grow up in regions where the ruling principle of the Universe is believed to be either capricious or hostile."[27] Three professors of quantum physics, Andrew Briggs, Hans Halvorson, and Andrew Steane (let's call them the 3Ps), have argued that "scientific understanding is valuable because it is part of our loving response to God, each other, and the wider world. It is a movement of the heart, and an outcome of the fact that God created the universe with the aim of producing beings who can love as He loves."[28]

This thesis may come as a surprise to people brought up on the received myths of conflict between Christian faith and science. People may raise various questions as to whether biblical faith really underlies the practice of the scientific enterprise. Some clarifications are needed at this point.

First, we are not arguing that Christians and their institutions underpinned the development of science, as if the label "Christian" automatically made someone or something scientific. Over their two-thousand-year history, Christians have been a mixed group of people. They have often expressed attitudes that are foreign to the gospel of Jesus, and have often been apathetic towards, or actively hostile to, scientific thinking. The (Christian) Galileo was opposed by the (Christian) philosophers in the universities. The (Christian) founders of the Royal Society were ridiculed by (Christian) skeptics who saw no value in their work.[29] As the science of geology developed in the 1800s, many of its early practitioners,[30] but not all of them,[31] accommodated their findings with their Christian faith. More recently, many American Christians have been vociferous in their denial of the threat of COVID-19 and in their rejection of vaccination, even as many others have

---

26. Briggs et al., *It Keeps Me Seeking*, 167.

27. Coulson, *Science and Christian Belief*, 80.

28. Briggs et al., *It Keeps Me Seeking*, 168.

29. Harrison, "Religion," 255–71.

30. Livingstone, *Darwin's Forgotten Defenders*, chs. 1, 3.

31. Holland, *Dominion*, ch. 18.

worked to develop vaccines and to promote their use.[32] Rather, the thesis claims that it is *the Bible's portrayal of God* and of *God's actions in history* that has been the foundation on which science has developed. The effect of the biblical revelation on many aspects of human endeavor has been at the level of *ideas*, of *imagination*, that have subverted and displaced prevailing mindsets.[33]

Second, it must be emphasized that many civilizations developed mathematics and technologies to high levels of sophistication, and made brilliant advances in scientific investigation, although these projects were not perpetuated, nor did they come to maturity in sustained research programs. Modern science has precedents in early modern and medieval thought, which was itself influenced by Arabic natural philosophy, which was in turn influenced by Greek, Egyptian, Indian, Persian, and Chinese texts. This has been called a "twisting braid" of scientific development.[34]

Francis Bacon, in the early 1600s, cited gunpowder, printing, and the compass as three world-changing technologies. All three had been developed in China before they were known in Europe.[35] Other technological advances in China were the production of cast-iron tools, sternpost rudders on ships, wrought-iron chains for suspension bridges, and the mechanical clock. Chinese astronomers provided the first recordings of sunspots and noted that the tails of comets pointed away from the sun. Medically, Chinese physicians used plant extracts containing ephedrine to suppress mucus production in the nose and discovered dietary approaches to treating beriberi.[36]

As far as science—the project to understand the workings of the natural world—is concerned, we must recognize the innovative scientific speculation and staggering advances of the ancient Greeks.[37] The study of the nature (*physis*, hence *physics*) of the world was conceived by the Greeks.[38] They sought "discoverable regularities in the natural world"; the Greek word *cosmos* meant *order*.[39] They developed the building materials

32. Whitehead and Perry, "How Culture Wars," 1–12.

33. A point argued by Nick Spencer, *Evolution*, 14, 16, 144–45.

34. Efron, "Myth 9," 85.

35. Wagner and Briggs, *Penultimate Curiosity*, xx.

36. Goodman and Russell, *Rise of Scientific Europe*, 9–11.

37. Worthing, *Unlikely Allies*, 35–43.

38. Jaki, *Science and Creation*, 102–4.

39. Goodman and Russell, *Rise of Scientific Europe*, 4.

of science: logic, mathematics, and a rational interpretation of the world.[40] They sought proof, developed empirical approaches to knowledge, and, in optics, studied "light as a department of geometry." Aristotle is known for his meticulous observational work, especially in biology.[41]

But their physics stagnated and ultimately atrophied because their worldview could not sustain it. Greek *physics* could not be sustained by Greek *metaphysics* (a word that came to mean knowledge *beyond physics*). David Bentley Hart has said that "The very notion that there was ever such a thing as ancient Greek or Roman 'science' in the modern sense is pure illusion."[42] Greek science included astrology, divination, the world-soul, the worship of deified heroes, and the belief in the divinity of the heavens. One of Greece's most influential thinkers, Aristotle, believed that all heavenly bodies above the moon—the planets, the Sun, and other stars—were perfect, animate, divine beings.[43]

In the fourth century, the theologian Basil of Caesarea, who was well schooled in Greek learning, proposed that the heavens, like the earth, are corruptible. It followed that the same laws of physics would apply to both the heavens and the earth.[44] The Christian John Philoponus believed the heavenly bodies to be fires and noted that they had different colors, just like fires on earth. He concluded that earthly and heavenly bodies were made of the same material. In this way he made the heretical assertion that the cosmos was one world. The pagan philosopher Simplicius condemned Philoponus for rejecting the divinity of the heavenly bodies—and this was as late as the sixth century.[45] Turner has said that scholars like Philoponus "broke from the ontology, epistemology and cosmology of the Greek dualist worldview, and replaced it with a more unified, relational and dynamic understanding that corresponds more closely to the way things actually are in the universe."[46]

The Greek worldview was based on the conviction that logic must rule; the heavens had to be rational and therefore perfect; and reality was unchanging. To Parmenides, change was an illusion. To the Stoics, the

40. Hooykaas, *Religion*, 85.

41. Goodman and Russell, *Rise of Scientific Europe*, 5.

42. Hart, *Atheist Delusions*, 67.

43. Turner, "Recasting," 154.

44. Kaiser, *Creation and the History of Science*, 5.

45. Kaiser, *Creation and the History of Science*, 13; Harrison, *Territories*, 53–54.

46. Turner, "Recasting," 165–66.

world passed through eternal recurrences. Plato responded to Parmenides by acknowledging that visible phenomena do change, but only because they are inadequate reflections of the ideal Forms of everything (blueprints that defined the natures of physical entities) that do not change. A consequence of Plato's thought is that sense data cannot be trusted. To the Epicureans, all was random and meaningless.[47]

Plato's creator (the *demiourgos*) was constrained by pre-existent matter. The *demiourgos* had to order (as well as he could) a chaotic, reasonless and recalcitrant matter, that was not of his creation. Aristotle's god, the Prime Mover, neither created the world, nor cared for it. Nature was like an organism that "makes everything to a final purpose." To Plato and Aristotle, the visible universe was itself a divine being. In people's efforts to understand the world, reason was preferred to experimentation.[48] Despite its spectacular heyday, Greek science could not progress because it lacked an appropriate sustaining metaphysical basis.

Clearly, many civilizations have shown intellectual brilliance, the elaboration of complex mathematics and ingenious technological innovation. These are the outcome of being human. But another ingredient—an enveloping and nurturing worldview—is needed before such skills can issue in scientific practice.

Third, we are *not* arguing that biblical faith is the source of the nuts and bolts of scientific methodology. The Hebrews were simple non-technological agriculturalists who had no science of their own. What we are saying is that science as a viable and self-sustaining activity arose from a union of the *physics* of the Greeks (and others) and the *metaphysics* of the Hebrews. Science is based on presuppositions—assumed unspoken understandings of reality—and these were assimilated from the faith of the ancient Hebrews. So Coulson states, "the presuppositions are such as to carry science, properly understood, into the realm of religion. For that common search for a common truth; that unexamined belief that facts are correlatable, i.e. stand in relation to one another and cohere in a scheme; that unprovable assumption that there is an 'order and constancy in Nature' . . . all of it is a legacy of religious conviction."[49] And when Coulson wrote of *religion*, he wrote as someone who believed in Jesus.

---

47. Judge, "Religion," 307; Jaki, *Science and Creation*, ch. 6.

48. Hooykaas, *Religion*, 1–6, 29–31.

49. Coulson, *Science and Christian Belief*, 75.

SCHOLARLY ASSESSMENTS

The message for people anxious about locating truth in an increasingly post-truth society is this: we must distinguish been *science* and the *nurturing presuppositions regarding reality* upon which science may flourish.[50] The human enterprise of science rests on the bedrock of biblical faith. The scientific world picture is founded upon the ancient Hebrew worldview. God is the source and guarantor of truth. Some summary statements from eminent scientists and historians show that the thesis presented here is not idiosyncratic opinion, but rests on the work and testimony of many learned scholars.

We have already quoted ancient historian Edwin Judge. He concluded that "It was not Greece, but Genesis, that has created modern science." Indeed, Judge continued: "In all three great dimensions of life—cosmic, social, and personal, the positions valued by secularists in particular stem from Jerusalem rather than Athens."[51] This might be a novelty to those fed Eurocentric formula from their infancy.

Medieval historian James Hannam said that "the natural philosophers of the Middle Ages . . . made science safe in a Christian context. . . . Their central belief that nature was created by God and so worthy of their attention was one that Galileo wholeheartedly endorsed. Without that awareness, modern science would simply not have happened."[52]

Philosopher and historian of science, Mark Worthing: "Contrary to popular perception, belief in one God and the natural sciences have been unlikely allies for over two millennia."[53] Worthing spoke of the "congruence of monotheistic and scientific thought."[54] Similarly, the Oxford historian of science Allan Chapman has said that "science as we know it stems from monotheism."[55]

The physicist and brain scientist Donald Mackay was renowned for his lucid explanations of issues at the science-theology interface. He stated that "logically and historically, science in our modern sense finds its greatest encouragement in the biblical doctrine of the natural world

---

50. Efron might have been more alert to the distinction between science and its enabling presuppositions; "Myth 9," 79–89.

51. Judge, "Religion of the Secularists," 307.

52. Hannam, *God's Philosophers*, 336.

53. Worthing, *Unlikely Allies*, 3.

54. Worthing, *Unlikely Allies*, 57.

55. Chapman, *Slaying the Dragons*, 13; also 17.

as God's creation."[56] A friend of MacKay's, geologist Frank Rhodes, was a distinguished president of Cornell University. He acknowledged that today people might accept the validity of the presuppositions of science (such as the order, regularity, and rationality of the universe) simply because science works. We now have centuries of precedent to go on. But the pioneers of science could make no such appeal to past successes. "They justified their assumptions on the basis of their belief in a personal, rational, and dependable God."[57]

Professor of physics (and theologian) John Polkinghorne argued that the Western Christian tradition approaches the physical world with "a commitment to reality, a search for rationality, and an acknowledgement of contingency" and he supports the thesis that "just such an ideological setting was the necessary matrix for the development of modern science."[58] In other words, science is possible because the universe is a creation.[59] To distinguished Harvard astronomer and historian of science Owen Gingerich, "the Judeo-Christian philosophical framework has proved to be a particularly fertile ground for the rise of modern science."[60] Another professor of physics, Tom McLeish, has written in the journal *Physics Today*: "The truth is that throughout most of history, scientific investigation has gone hand in hand with a commitment to theism."[61] With another physicist, David Hutchings, McLeish has argued that the truth, often drowned out by the noise, is "that science flows naturally from the Christian worldview and that it always has."[62] And our three professors (3Ps) have stated that "belief in God is a presupposition of scientific practice."[63] Steane has himself stated that science was born in a context of theism (where *theism* is belief in a self-revealing God): "the birthplace of empirical science was theistically devout—devout in a seriously committed way, not just following social conventions of the time."[64] The 1600s were marked by particularly vigor-

56. MacKay, *Science and the Quest*, 39.

57. Rhodes, "Christianity," 18–19.

58. Polkinghorne, *Reason and Reality*, 74.

59. Polkinghorne, *Beyond Science*, 92.

60. Gingerich, *God's Universe*, 6.

61. McLeish, "Thinking Differently," 10–12.

62. Hutchings and McLeish, *Let There Be Science*, 10; also 11, 14, 45, 59, 60, 166, 168.

63. Briggs et al., *It Keeps Me Seeking*, 169.

64. Steane, *Faithful to Science*, 33.

ous development of early modern science (called natural philosophy at that time) and particularly strong interest in the theology-science interface.[65]

Harold Turner expressed the relation in a slightly different way. He saw the roots of science and the roots of Christianity as being intertwined. Both in fact arose from Hebrew thinking as it developed over the two thousand years leading up to the time of Jesus.[66] Turner wrote of "the Christian doctrine of the created world . . . as providing the basic worldview and metaphysics necessary for the work of science."[67] The roots of science are to be located on a bedrock of a biblically informed worldview. On the one hand, science needed emancipation from Greek theology. On the other hand, it needed to adopt Judeo-Christian theology, and this theology was "first developed among the Hebrews." Turner stated that the differences in the Greek and biblical worldviews represent "sharp alternatives, not matters of degree."[68]

Turner recognized, however, that the biblical worldview was necessary but not sufficient for the development of science. Science needed other conditions, such as decimals from China and India, Arabic enumeration, and technologies for accurate timekeeping. Stable social and political conditions were needed in the mix too,[69] and the growth of maritime exploration and commerce also encouraged scientific thinking.[70]

65. Osler, "Myth 10," 90–98.
66. Turner, "Recasting," 149.
67. Turner, "Recasting," 164.
68. Turner, "Recasting," 165.
69. Turner, "Recasting," 166.
70. Efron, "Myth 9," 85–86.

2

ONE SOURCE OF CREATION

IT IS EASY TO overlook the sheer novelty of the biblical concept of *creation*. In reality, the postulate of creation—that a creator God is the source of all being—was a radical innovation in human thought. C. S. Lewis wrote:

> The Jews, as we all know, believed in one God, maker of heaven and earth. Nature and God were distinct; the One had made the other; the One ruled and the other obeyed.... I suspect that many people assume that some clear doctrine of creation underlies all religions: that in Paganism the gods, or one of the gods, usually created the world; even that religions normally begin by asking the question, "Who made the world?" In reality, creation, in any unambiguous sense, seems to be a surprisingly rare doctrine.[1]

The Hebrew (biblical) concept of creation was a revolutionary new insight in human awareness and the source of particular presuppositions that facilitated the development of scientific thinking. Alexander observes that "the Greek passion for logic and mathematics was baptized into a biblical framework of creation," producing a new synthesis that stimulated the development of modern science.[2] Several science-facilitating corollaries of the biblical idea of creation will be discussed in this chapter. But first, the concept of creation should be placed into the widest human context.

Harold Turner has described how, over human history, people have entertained three basic understandings of reality (Fig. 2). First, the *tribal religions* conceived of their world—gods, spirits, ancestors, sorcerers and

1. Lewis, *Reflections*, 67.
2. Alexander, *Rebuilding the Matrix*, 91.

their magic, physical and biological processes—as constituting one living ("encapsulated") whole. This primal view was animistic and pantheistic. There was no consistency or coherence in the natural order, and such cosmologies could never sustain the development of science.

Second, the *axial religions* of Greece and Asia developed around the sixth century BC as reactions against the monistic tribal worldview. The divine element (which was depersonalized) and the material element (often seen as a prison of the soul) were often radically separated from each other in a dualistic system. Dichotomies arose between spirit and matter, mind and body, intellect and the senses, theory and practice, essence and appearance. In each pair, the former feature was favored over the latter. In other words, concrete physical reality was devalued, and impulses to developing scientific investigation of that reality were thereby suppressed.

Third, the ancient Hebrew tribes from the second millennium BC developed the idea of a rational and faithful creator God, in constant and purposive relationship with God's world. In this view, an interacting duality (as distinct from a noninteracting dualism) of creator and creation guaranteed the orderliness and consistency of material reality and facilitated rational exploration of it.[3] This unique tribal understanding and its further developments in Christian faith will be explored in the following sections.

3. I first heard Turner's thesis in a seminar entitled "Science and Religion," Centre for Continuing Education, University of Auckland, 23 March 1996. It was summarized in Turner, "Religion: Impediment or Saviour," 155–64. Monistic, dualistic, and duality worldviews are discussed in Turner, *Roots*, 21–78.

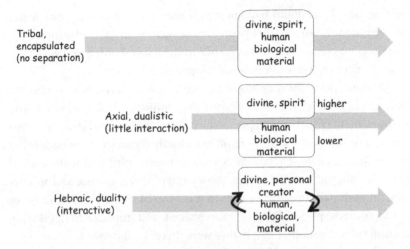

Fig. 2. Relating the divine and the world
Turner has described human religions as falling into three categories: the tribal
"encapsulated" or monistic view, the stark non-interactive dualism of the Axial religions,
and the interactive God-creation duality of the Hebraic.

GOD IS ALMIGHTY

The Old Testament scholar Gordon Wenham has emphasized the importance to scientific thinking of the first chapter of the book of Genesis. This
text asserts that there is "one almighty God who created and controls the
world according to a coherent plan." This foundational belief supports an
"assumption of unity and order underlying the manifold and seemingly capricious phenomena of experience." It follows that "Only such an assumption can justify the experimental method. Were this world controlled by a
multitude of capricious deities, or subject to mere chance, no consistency
could be expected in experimental results, and no scientific laws could be
discovered." Genesis 1 has thus "provided the intellectual underpinning of
the scientific enterprise."[4]

Those who placed their confidence in the God of Genesis did not
share in the terrors of peoples who lived under the panoply of nature gods.
The fertility rites of the Babylonian Akitu festival were permeated with "a
fear that order, cosmic and social, may fall prey at any time to chaos."[5]
The Aztecs and Carthaginians lived in fear that reality might dissolve into

4. Wenham, *Genesis 1–15*, 39.
5. Jaki, *Science and Creation*, 95.

nothingness. "To secure the uninterrupted recurrence of nature's cycles constituted a foremost objective for the Aztecs."[6] People who hold these views live in a pervasive state of anxiety.

But Israel's God had no competitors. There was no one who could undermine or undo God's creative work. The biblical worldview is not dualist: this God never had to combat equal and opposite forces of evil. The ancient Israelites and their spiritual heirs were free of any anxiety that they lived in a cosmic lottery or that the world might collapse into chaos. Jaki's description of Genesis chapter 1 leaves no doubt as to its fruitfulness for science. "For all the Mesopotamian flavor of Genesis 1, its author uses the common lore with unusual skill to drive home some very uncommon points. These are the absolute sovereignty and precedence of God over any and all parts of the world, the infinite power of God who brings things into existence with sheer command, and his overflowing goodness."[7]

If God is creator of the cosmos—of every physical entity of which we can conceive—then God is the guarantor of its continuing reality and of the truth regarding its nature. People may be assured that there are valid ways of describing the universe and its components, because they are sustained as *objective realities* that are *independent* of us, and they will not compromise with our cultural preconditioning, preconceptions, preferences, and prejudices. The universe is constituted in a particular way, and scientists set out to discover what that is.

The emphasis on truth provides an expectation that there is an underlying objective reality to our world, and that this is discoverable. C. A. Coulson said, "the presuppositions underlying all scientific effort, are often, though not always, unexamined by the scientist. These, when they were uncovered, were seen to involve a belief in the universal character of truth, in what our prayer book calls the 'order and constancy of Nature.'"[8]

Donald MacKay said that "belief in 'truth' or 'ultimate reality' is appropriate because God has made himself the guarantor of such things."[9] The "ideal of objectivity is one to which anyone who believes in the Christian God of truth is committed as a matter of religions duty."[10] More specifically, Christian theism "more powerfully and coherently than any other

6. Jaki, *Science and Creation*, 50–51 and ch.3.

7. Jaki, *Science and Creation*, 147.

8. Coulson, *Science and Christian Belief*, 84.

9. In Thorson, "Scientific Objectivity," 73.

10. MacKay, "Objectivity," 15.

intellectual mind frame sets objectivity before us as an ultimate value to be cherished and aspired to as part of our loving duty to our Creator."[11] Regardless of how confused or off-target our thinking may be, there is a divine Author "who knows the way things are, for it is he who created them."[12] So we should not despair of our ignorance or the limitations of our rationality: the objective truth of the world is guaranteed, and we can expect to learn more about it as we observe and experiment.

GOD'S WISDOM GIVES ORDER TO THE COSMOS

People who recognize a pantheon of competing gods, or a rabble of gods who must struggle to impose order on an independent physical substrate, will hardly have confidence that the world is structured in a way that is coherent and comprehensible. But the Bible presents creation as a "divine speech-act." This means that creation is not an emanation from God, nor is it the capricious outcome of the random activities of competing gods. It is an expression of God's thoughts and is essentially intelligible.[13]

To the founders of science, the world was rationally ordered and intelligible. The great scientists of the 1600s (Boyle, Newton) "thought that the underlying patterns and order present in the physical world were there because they had been created by a rational divine mind."[14] They were informed by the people (for example) who wrote the first chapter of Genesis, which provides "a most lucid expression of that faith in the rationality of the universe without which the scientific quest in man could not turn itself into a self-sustaining enterprise."[15] The creation story of Genesis 1 describes God's imposition of order on creation. The text progresses from chaos to cosmos.

As the Christian chemist and philosopher Walter Thorson expressed it: "Since God is in heaven, the world is rational."[16] Philosopher Roger Trigg has said that, "As a matter of historical fact, modern science has developed from an understanding of the world as God's ordered creation, with its own

11. MacKay, "Objectivity," 17.

12. MacKay, "Objectivity," 18, 23.

13. Osborn, *Guardians*, 109.

14. Trigg, "Does Science Need Religion?" 21.

15. Jaki, *Science and Creation*, 146.

16. Thorson, "Spiritual Dimensions," 230.

inherent rationality."[17] Theologian David Bentley Hart has stated that "belief in God, properly understood, allows one to see all that exists—both in its own being and in our knowledge of it—as rational."[18] Mark Worthing has stated, "If the mind of God is coherent and comprehensible, then the world which God creates will also be coherent and comprehensible; thus it can be approached and investigated with the expectation that it can be understood."[19]

Charles Coulson considered that the coherence and interpretability of the universe reflect mind: "there seems but one source for its origin. It must come from the medieval insistence of the rationality of God."[20] As an example, Coulson quoted the physicist Johann Balmer (1885), who sought "divine orderliness" in wavelengths of emitted light from discharge tubes of hydrogen gas.[21] And the contemporary quantum mechanical 3Ps state that: "If it is indeed the case that God created the universe, then to acknowledge this doesn't serve as an alternative to going into the laboratory. Rather, it tells us that it's worthwhile to go into the laboratory. The statement that God is creator presents an encouragement to explore, and it holds out a promise that the universe is intelligible, and our labors to understand it are not in vain."[22]

A person does not have to possess Christian faith to recognize the essential compatibility of theological belief with nature's order. The cosmologist Paul Davies has said, "Science can proceed only if the scientist adopts an essentially theological worldview . . . even the most atheistic scientist accepts as an act of faith the existence of a law-like order in nature that is at least in part comprehensible to us."[23] It is a pity that more secular scientists do not reflect more deeply into the (hidden) worldview from which empirical research disciplines have arisen.

---

17. Trigg, "Does Science Need Religion?" 22.

18. Hart, *Experience*, 236.

19. Worthing, *Unlikely Allies*, 52.

20. A. N. Whitehead, quoted in Coulson, *Science and Christian Belief*, 76; in Worthing, *Unlikely Allies*, 52–53.

21. Coulson, *Science and Christian Belief*, 77.

22. Briggs, Halvorson, and Steane, *It Keeps Me Seeking*, 174.

23. http://hyperphysics.phy-astr.gsu.edu/Nave-html/Faithpathh/Davies.html. I thank Dr. Zachary Ardern for informing me of this comment.

GOD IS FAITHFUL

One of the sources of Israel's joy and confidence was that God is faithful. And if God is faithful, the processes of the world must be lawful and consistent. Physical reality will behave consistently through time and space. Physicist Tom McLeish has pointed out[24] that in the "greatest ancient nature poem," Job 38–40, the lawfulness of nature has already been promulgated: "Do you know the laws of the heavens? Can you set up God's dominion over the earth?"[25]

In this typically Hebrew parallelism, "the laws of the heavens" are linked with "God's dominion." C. S. Lewis has famously said "Men became scientific because they expected Law in Nature, and they expected Law in Nature because they believed in a Legislator."[26] A deeply rooted belief in that divine Legislator predisposed Bible readers to the practice of science.

As Hannam says, "The starting point for all natural philosophy in the Middle Ages was that nature had been created by God. This made it a legitimate area of study because, through nature, man could learn about its creator. Medieval scholars thought that nature followed the rules God had ordained for it. Because God was consistent and not capricious, these natural laws were constant and worth scrutinizing."[27]

Over a century ago, Pierre Duhem, the pioneer historian of science, claimed that "the unification of the universe with one set of laws was a direct result of Christian theology." Yet Aristotelianism was not quickly abandoned, and the theologian Eric Mascall wondered whether Duhem had overstated his case—but added that we can fully agree that this expectation of universal law "ought to have been" the result of Christian theology![28] We are often slow to perceive the implications of biblical theology.

According to the historian of science Peter Harrison, "The idea, first proposed in the seventeenth century, that nature was governed by mathematical laws, was directly informed by theological considerations."[29] Not only did Newton discover laws of nature, but more foundationally, was convinced that such laws actually existed, and awaited discovery. In the

24. McLeish, "What Is Science?".

25. Job 38:33 (NIV). The GNT reads, "Do you know the laws that govern the skies, and can you make them apply to the earth?"

26. Lewis, *Miracles*, 128.

27. Hannam, *God's Philosophers*, 340.

28. Russell, *Cross-Currents*, 67.

29. Harrison, "Christianity," 17.

seventeenth century, medieval belief in God's legislative moral power was extended to the physical world. "God's authorship of the laws of nature guaranteed their universality and unchanging nature."[30]

Plato's philosophy emphasized the importance of approaching the world in a mathematical way. That perspective influenced later natural philosophers. Pioneering physicists such as Galileo, Kepler, Descartes, and Newton "were convinced that mathematical truths were not the products of human minds, but of the divine mind. God was the source of mathematical relations that were evident in the laws of the universe."[31] Gingerich emphasizes the same point. "In fact, the very expression 'laws of nature,' from the time of Boyle and Newton, derives from the concept of divine law, and it is probably not accidental that science arose in such a philosophical/theological environment."[32]

Roger Penrose, agnostic and mathematician, stated that "There is something absolute and 'God-given' about mathematical truth. . . . Not only is the universe 'out there' but mathematical truth has its own independence and timelessness."[33] Agnostics and Christians use the word *God* in different ways. But add to Penrose's idea of *God* "the one who loves and will renew creation by sending Jesus as God's perfect self-expression or Word," and Penrose's statement encapsulates biblical faith perfectly.

To the twenty-first-century Christian, the relationship between the faithfulness of God and the laws of nature is perhaps more nuanced. Natural laws are not *prescriptive* but *descriptive*. God does not *decree* how matter should behave; rather, God's utter faithfulness, his dependability, his reliability in the way he sustains reality, are manifested in the consistency of the world. The laws of nature are the ways we formulate and codify the perfect constancy with which God upholds created reality.[34] Donald MacKay has said: "This biblical concept of our world as a world of created events, cohering to precedent because their Creator is faithful to a pattern, positively encourages the sort of expectations that we call 'scientific.'"[35] As such, the laws of nature are not set in stone but may be modified with the growth of human knowledge. Newton's law of gravity was not the final, unalterable

---

30. Harrison, "Christianity," 18; also Brooke, *Science and Religion*, 19.

31. Harrison, "Christianity," 19–21.

32. Gingerich, *God's Universe*, 71–72.

33. As quoted by a fellow Oxonian, Houghton, *Search for God*, 203.

34. MacKay, *Clockwork Image*, 31–32, 60.

35. MacKay, *Science and the Quest*, 44.

statement of the subject, but provided an excellent approximation until the formulation of Einstein's more complete understanding (as described by general relativity) about three centuries later.

GOD ACTS IS FREEDOM

Plato and Aristotle believed that the true nature of reality was enshrined in eternal concepts (the so-called *Ideas* and *Forms*) and that the actions of the gods were constrained by these abstractions. The pioneers of science recognized that God is free. God was not limited or restricted by any principles beyond God's own self. In contrast to Plato's divine *demiourgos*, God acts and creates in freedom. As a result, the world is *contingent*. It means that, from our vantage point, reality does not *have* to be the way it is. It could have been structured differently. This understanding has several important corollaries. We cannot do our science by starting with self-evident axioms, and then deducing from them how the world is structured and how it operates. Pure deduction was the ancient Greek ideal. That approach is called *rationalism*, and it has never contributed anything to science. Rather, if God is free and the world is contingent, we can understand that world only by careful observation and experimentation. "That's the bit the Greeks missed," as Polkinghorne put it.[36] Science requires open-minded *empiricality*—close attention to the way the world is—with an attendant *rationality*, by which the data of experience are analyzed.

The Greeks emphasized logical deduction from self-evident first principles. By contrast, "modern science was unlocked from mere logic by the empiricism of personal experience as tested in Jerusalem"—that is, according to the Judeo-Christian worldview. The appeal to personal experience, based on empirical testing, represents "the refutation of the Aristotelian universe." The Greek physician and philosopher Galen (second century) rejected the experimental method because it lacked logical proof. It was too much like "the school of Moses and Christ."[37] And yet it is attention to the particularities and vicissitudes of history that facilitates empirical approaches to reality. An unexpected anomaly can often lead into a whole new field of knowledge (see chapter 5 on the counter-intuitiveness of Christian theology and science).

36. Polkinghorne, *Quarks*, 18.
37. Judge, "Religion," 307.

To quote Gingerich, "One of the great ideas of the Judeo-Christian tradition is the notion of God's freedom (and hence the contingency of nature), which has provided a rich philosophical ground for the rise of modern science. Since God could have made the universe in many different ways . . . it behooves the scientist to undertake experiments or observations to find out which way in fact characterizes the universe."[38] The concept is subtle but foundational and is emphasized by many scholars.[39]

GOD IS CREATOR: CREATION IS DE-DIVINIZED (OR DE-DEIFIED)

According to biblical faith, God has no peers, and (*contra* Plato and Aristotle!) all that is not God is created by God. The biblical idea of creation entails that the world and everything in it come from God. The creation concept is introduced in Genesis chapter 1, which is an attack on ancient Near-Eastern nature cults. The sun, moon and stars are not gods, but lights set in the sky by the creator. God blesses creation, indicating that it is not divine—nature is *de-divinized*—and its fertility is not an autonomous capacity but a gift.[40]

This concept of creation has major implications. As C. S. Lewis has said, "the doctrine of creation in one sense empties nature of divinity."[41] All forms of animism, pantheism, or polytheism are excluded from the biblical worldview, but that does not reduce creation to mere commodity to be exploited according to human whim. "By emptying nature of divinity—or, let us say, of divinities—you may fill her with Deity, for she is now the bearer of messages."[42] Nature is *not* God nor is it a *part of* God, but constantly *owes its origins* to God. Nature *belongs to* God, is *"infused"* with God (that is, God is *immanent* in it), and *points us* to God.

The Bible roundly rejected all notions that nature is pervaded and controlled by occult forces or magic—notions that still endure as ideas

---

38. Gingerich, *God's Universe*, 116

39. Hooykaas, *Religion*, 31, 47; Polkinghorne, *Reason and Reality*, 74; Turner, *Roots of Science*, 59–62; Trigg, *Beyond Matter*, 79, 86, 92–93, 96; Trigg, "Does Science Need Religion?" 20.

40. Osborn, *Guardians*, 85.

41. Lewis, *Reflections*, 69.

42. Lewis, *Reflections*, 71; also MacKay, *Science and the Quest*, 10–12.

hostile to science.[43] In addition, Hooykaas (along with many others) has argued that "There is a radical contrast between the deification of nature in pagan religion and, in a rationalized form, in Greek philosophy, and the de-deification of nature in the Bible."[44] To the Hebrews, the sky, the rivers and the trees are not inhabited by gods, spirits or fairies. The physical world is not divine. The world is *de-deified* or *de-divinized*. This is not to say that nature is *de-sacralized*. The world remains sacred to Christians because it belongs to God and is the realm of God's continued action and purpose. The world is not to be exploited or otherwise abused by humanity.[45] Our moral responsibilities in a de-deified but sacred creation are discussed more fully in chapter 6.

Mark Worthing has argued similarly. Ancient pagan thought, including that of the Greeks, had "little concept of secularity."[46] Monotheistic faith was entirely different, because "gods, spirits, and magic were taken out of rocks, trees, and hills. . . . As sacrality became centralized in the being of God, particularly the Judeo-Christian God, the physical world itself became secularized. . . . An emerging natural science was no longer faced with the daunting task of challenging a sacred world filled with spirits, gods, holy places and holy people."[47] (Worthing's use of *sacrality/sacred* might have been better rendered as *divinity/divine*, as indicated above.) Science could no longer be seen as an invasion of the privacy of supernatural personal agencies. In other words, the biblical concept of creation gave people the freedom to investigate nature. As Polkinghorne expressed it, "because creation is not itself divine, we can prod it and investigate it without impiety."[48]

The biblical distinction between God and a de-deified world has had major ramifications for the scientific mindset. We are free to ask questions of nature because we are not invading the privacy of spirits or gods. "Monotheism by its very nature encouraged the asking of questions about the functions of the natural world."[49] Indeed, the "primary creative grammar" of science "is the question, rather than the answer."[50] In the climax of

---

43. Thorson, "Spiritual Dimensions," 225–27; Hart, *Atheist Delusions*, 232–33.

44. Hooykaas, *Religion*, 7; Turner, *Roots*, 62–78; Konig, *New and Greater Things*, 75.

45. Bauckham, *Bible and Ecology*, 85–86.

46. Worthing, *Unlikely Allies*, 48.

47. Worthing, *Unlikely Allies*, 49–50; Turner, *Roots*, ch. 4.

48. Polkinghorne, *Quarks*, 18.

49. Worthing, *Unlikely Allies*, 50.

50. McLeish, *Faith*, 102; also 53, 190–96, 263.

the biblical book of Job, God is said to issue a barrage of questions about the natural world. According to Tom McLeish, scientific colleagues read these chapters with astonishment and delight. The questions that constituted God's challenge to Job provide the "primary questions" that underlie the range of scientific fields from cosmology to zoology.[51] The questions point us to both a gift and an invitation. We are *given* the capacities to enquire into, and reason about, the world; and we are *invited* to do so, to become reconciled with both the "wondrous creation'" around us, and with "the Creator himself."[52]

The sociologist Toby Huff has drawn attention to the inquisitiveness that characterized many people in Europe. The invention of the telescope sparked intense astronomical investigation in the West, but not in China or in the Muslim world.[53] Is this curiosity linked to the biblical invitation to inquire of nature?

GOD IS HOLY

C. S. Lewis describes how, long ago, humans developed a *sense of awe*, reflecting an awareness of the Numinous, of the Divine.[54] In addition to that, humans came to experience a *sense of the moral*.[55] But a

> third stage in religious development arises when men identify them—when the Numinous Power to which they feel awe is made the guardian of the morality to which they feel obligation. . . . Of all the jumps that humanity takes in its religious history this is certainly the most surprising. . . . Perhaps only a single people, as a people, took the new step with perfect decision—I mean the Jews, . . . and only those who take it are safe from the obscenities and barbarities of unmoralised worship or the cold, sad self-righteousness of sheer moralism. . . . [I]t was the Jews who fully and unambiguously identified the awful Presence haunting black mountain-tops and thunderclouds with "the *righteous* Lord" who "loveth righteousness."[56]

---

51. McLeish, *Faith*, 105.

52. Hutchings and McLeish, *Let There Be Science*, 57–58.

53. Huff, *Intellectual Curiosity*.

54. Lewis, *Problem*, 4–9.

55. Lewis, *Problem*, 9–10.

56. Lewis, *Problem*, 10–11.

Deeply embedded in Israel's story is the conviction that her God is the God of *truth*. In the core of Israel's prophetic scriptures, we read: "I, the LORD, speak the truth; I declare what is right."[57] The history of Jesus continued the same emphasis on the moral imperative that is truth. "Grace and truth came through Jesus Christ."[58] Jesus flummoxed the Roman Governor Pontius Pilate during his interrogation when he told Pilate that he "came for this one purpose, to speak about the truth"—the truth about God's wise (peaceful) ordering of this world,[59] a concept to which Pilate could not relate. St. Paul urged his readers to emulate the truth that is found in Jesus,[60] for it is "by speaking the truth in a spirit of love we must grow up in every way to Christ."[61]

The biblical emphasis on *God's truth* has important consequences for science. The practice of science requires that the investigators are committed to truthfulness in the sense of *moral integrity*. Their gathering, analysis, and reporting of data must be performed *objectively*. Their work cannot be tainted by what they might hope to find. The divine characteristic of truthfulness requires people to do their scientific work ethically, with impartiality and integrity. An awareness of righteousness and truth underlies scientific progress. Truth in God and the objective reality of nature requires truthfulness in the investigator.[62]

Coulson expands on this theme: "Theodor Mommsen's famous phrase 'science without presuppositions' is a hopelessly superficial description of our discipline." Coulson proceeds to list values that must precede the work of any scientist:

> there is honesty and integrity and hope: there is enthusiasm, for no one ever yet began an experiment without an element of passion: . . . there is a humility before a created order of things, which are to be received and studied: . . . there is co-operation with his fellows, both in the same laboratory, and across the seven seas: there is patience, akin to that which kept Mme Curie at her self-imposed task of purifying eight tons of pitchblende to extract the few odd milligrams of radium: above all there is judgment. . . . Not only do we believe that there *is* a truth, and that this truth is accessible to all

57. Isa 45:19.

58. John 1:17.

59. John 18:37; Wright, *How God Became King*, 144, 230.

60. Eph 4:21.

61. Eph 4:15.

62. Alexander, *Rebuilding the Matrix*, 244–45.

people; but equally we know what is good or bad science, whether in experiment or theory, and we adopt towards our publication the highest conceivable standards of integrity."[63]

The moral qualities needed to do science are not a part of science. Nor does honesty come naturally to scientists, as if they are more truthful than non-scientists. Integrity is a presupposition, a system of imperatives, that comes to people from their understanding about the moral structure of the universe, and ultimately from the God who is its source. Indeed, small changes in the baseline of moral integrity in society can have large implications for the practice of science (as discussed, chapter 4).[64]

CREATION IS GOOD

Many cultures have lacked the conviction that physical reality is good. The people of the Mesopotamian superpowers Sumer, Assyria, and Babylon (Israel's threatening neighbors) labored under a pessimistic outlook on the world.[65] In brilliant contrast, Israel's God declared his creative work (very) good (Genesis 1)—it was eminently fit for God's purposes.[66] Significantly, "non-human creatures are unequivocally stated to be good without reference to humankind. . . . The creature is good (and, hence, beautiful) by virtue of its standing in appropriate relationship to its creator."[67] Creatures are not good because we can sentimentalize them, exploit them, or commodify them. They are good because God evaluates them as such.

To the ancient Hebrew prophets, matter mattered—it had a future. "The whole earth is full of [God's] glory."[68] Even when evil was oppressive and pervasive, the Hebrew people could rejoice that "the earth will be filled with the knowledge of the glory of the LORD as the waters cover the sea."[69] Israel's wisdom literature reflected on the chanciness of the world but spoke gladly of the divinely given order that was everywhere apparent. When Job felt overwhelmed by accident and evil at the micro-level he inhabited, he

63. Coulson, *Science and Christian Belief*, 72–75.

64. See Oreskes and Conway, *Merchants* (discussed later) for insights into the effects of non-truth on science.

65. Jaki, *Science and Creation*, ch. 5.

66. Konig, *New and Greater Things*, 159, 166.

67. Osborn, *Guardians*, 86.

68. Isa 6:3 (NIV); Thorson, "Spiritual Dimensions," 255–56.

69. Hab 2:14; Wright, *Surprised by Scripture*, 22, 201.

was told to consider the emergent wonder of God's creation—cosmological, meteorological, biological—as it functioned at the macro-level. As mentioned earlier, Tom McLeish has proposed that the flood of questions in the book of Job pointing to nature's wonders facilitated scientific thinking.[70]

Hart emphasizes how Greek and Roman culture was deeply melancholic. It was characterized by spiritual despondency. "It was pagan society that had become ever more otherworldly and joyless, ever wearier of the burden of itself, and ever more resentful of the soul's incarceration in the closed system of a universe governed by fate . . . and that could imagine no philosophical virtue more impressive than resignation to the impossibility of escape."[71] In contrast, the Christian church proclaimed "far more radically than any other ancient system of thought, the incorruptible goodness of the world, the original and ultimate beauty of all things, inasmuch as it understood this world to be the direct creation of the omnipotent God of love."[72] The world was a source of delight—how could people who saw it as God's gift fail to investigate it? Hart again: the world was seen "as a gratuitous work of transcendent love . . . to be received with gratitude, delighted in as an act of divine pleasure, mourned as a victim of human sin, admired as a radiant manifestation of divine glory."[73]

St Paul, an early (Jewish) disciple of Jesus, could stress "without a shadow of pagan or pantheistic divinizing of creation, that food is good, marriage and sex are good, the created order is good, and that humans ought to enjoy them as what they are—that is, as parts of God's good creation."[74] Paul wholly rejected pagan dualism, which sometimes suggested that the world and human bodies are evil, so should be avoided. We are at liberty to enjoy God's world, and that freedom is precisely what the pioneers of science engaged in.

Christianity in particular makes claims that establish once and for ever the value of physical creation. In the incarnation, "the Word became flesh"[75]—in other words, the self-expressing God became a biological creature—an anthropoid primate, a human being, Jesus of Nazareth. Given the biblical distinction between the creator and the ever-dependent creation,

70. McLeish, *Faith*, 102–6.

71. Hart, *Atheist Delusions*, 143–44.

72. Hart, *Atheist Delusions*, 144.

73. Hart, *Atheist Delusions*, 212.

74. Wright and Bird, *New Testament in Its World*, 372.

75. John 1:14.

the idea that divinity should become embodied in created materiality comes as a colossal surprise—and one that emphasizes the supreme value of creation to God. God has become joined to created matter.

Central to Christian faith is the resurrection of Jesus, to be shared by those who are united to him.[76] Polkinghorne has written that "the pattern that is me will be remembered by God and recreated by him in some new environment of his choosing in his ultimate act of resurrection." But the biblical hope is that *all* of creation will share in this sublime destiny. "The universe is going to die but, because God cares for it, it will have its resurrection beyond its death, just as we shall have our resurrection beyond our deaths. In fact, the two destinies are one."[77] To emphasize that Polkinghorne's view is not excessively colored by his physics, we quote Tom Wright. Resurrection is the "reaffirmation of the universe of space, time and matter, . . . the action of the creator god to reaffirm the essential goodness of creation, . . . an initial and representative act of new creation."[78]

In the resurrection, physical reality is taken up into the eternal life of God. Resurrection is the first step in new creation. The world we live in is scheduled to be transformed. It is not to be discarded, or trashed, but redeemed from its bondage to decay.[79] Physical reality has God-given value. It is worthy of reverent and wondering investigation. It follows that belief in the resurrection of Jesus also provides powerful motivation to creation care (as will be reiterated in the context of motivations to sustainability, chapter 6). To exploit and deface nature for the sake of accumulating trinkets or gratifying our uncontrollable appetites for pleasure is a repellent crime. The solemn warning that God will "destroy those who destroy the earth"[80] speaks to our current situation of rampant ecological abuse. And it re-emphasizes the enduring value of creation to God.

At the dawn of the scientific revolution in the 1600s, "the notion that ordinary matter could repay the attention of men of learning seemed absurd to many people." But a few people considered that if "God thought matter worth creating [and indeed redeeming], then they might find it

76. 1 Cor 15:20–23; Rom 8:11; Phil 3:20–21.

77. Polkinghorne, *Beyond Science*, 100.

78. Wright, *Resurrection*, 729–30.

79. Rom 8:19–23.

80. Rev 11:18.

worth studying, and might expect to be rewarded by finding order and harmony in the most commonplace objects and events."[81]

GOD SPEAKS

Everywhere in the Hebrew Scriptures, God addresses his people. What "the LORD says," together with the human requirement to listen, is a recurring theme of the prophets. For example:

> The LORD says, "Listen now, Israel, my servant,
> My chosen people, the descendants of Jacob.
> I am the LORD who created you;
> From the time you were born I have helped you."[82]

Congruent with the supreme importance of the spoken word in the divine address, God's ultimate communication was addressed to humanity in the form of his embodied word, Jesus:

> In the beginning the Word already existed; the Word was with God and the Word was God. From the very beginning the Word was with God. . . . The Word became a human being and, full of grace and truth, lived among us.[83]

It follows that, as Walter Thorson expresses it, "in Hebrew culture, the dominant epistemological [knowledge-gaining] motif is that of hearing and listening."[84] The Protestant Reformation laid great emphasis on the importance of listening, "with its emphasis upon hearing the word of God, and letting it speak to us . . . and upon the obedience of the mind in response to it."[85] The mindset of listening was an expression of faith in the character of God.

Jesus said that it was necessary to be like a child to enter the kingdom of heaven.[86] The pioneer philosopher of science Francis Bacon echoed Jesus's admonition when he stated, "The entry into the kingdom of man, founded on the sciences, is not very different from the entry into the kingdom of

---

81. MacKay, *Clockwork Image*, 24.
82. Isa 44:1–2.
83. John 1:1–5, 10, 14.
84. Thorson, "Scientific Objectivity," 75.
85. Thorson, "Scientific Objectivity," 76.
86. Mark 10:15/Luke 18:17; Matt 18:3.

heaven, whereinto none may enter save as a little child." Over two centuries later the agnostic T. H. Huxley also applied the teaching of Jesus to the scientific attitude when he stated that the scientist should sit down before the facts like a child.[87] We cannot expect either God or the natural world to comply with our expectations. To force our prejudices upon the "other" is to render us insensible to its illumination.

The importance of listening has clear implications for the practice of science. It "places epistemological stress on our being receptive or responsive to what comes to us from the Other."[88] In both theology and in science, to cultivate an attitude of listening is to "stand under" the reality that is there and "to allow it to shape my knowing in response to it. Implicit in this attitude is the conviction that objective reality will 'speak' to those who listen."[89]

GOD IS REDEEMING

We have already alluded to the prevailing notion held by many ancient Greek thinkers that the world undergoes repeating cycles of dissolution and rebirth.[90] Stanley Jaki has described how many civilizations—Indian, Mesoamerican, Egyptian, Mesopotamian, Greek—subscribed to a belief in cosmic returns.[91] This notion of the unending treadmill of time could be psychologically dispiriting and it also minimized the significance of time and of cause-effect relationships that occurred in time.

The revolution in the understanding of time occurred in the faith of one people. Theologian Adrio Konig has said that "Israel developed the *linear* concept of time and of history." History has a starting point and proceeds to a terminus or goal.[92] Biblical faith was based on the belief that God has acted (and still acts) in history. "God has revealed himself as a person with a history embedded in the history of the human race and the cosmos as a whole."[93] David Bentley Hart has said that to believe in the *arrow of time*—that is, to "believe in history[—]is to assume that human time

87. Houghton, *Search for God*, 203.

88. Thorson, "Scientific Objectivity," 76.

89. Thorson, "Scientific Objectivity," 77.

90. Judge, "Religion of the Secularists," 307.

91. Jaki, *Science and Creation*, chs. 1, 3, 4, 5, 6 respectively.

92. Konig, *New and Greater Things*, 78, 167–68.

93. Osborn, *Guardians*, 106.

obeys a certain narrative logic, one that accommodates both disjunction and resolution and that moves towards an end quite different from its beginning."[94] Hart stated that pagan peoples did not have this sense of history: for them, human history was simply part of the cycles of nature. All was ultimately meaningless. But faith in Jesus "gave history not only a meaning but also an absolute significance, as it was within time that the entire drama of fall, incarnation, and salvation had been and was being worked out."[95]

Harold Turner has said that, for Israel, "Historical time has been redeemed from its rejection as in almost all other faiths. It is now treated as the scene of the divine presence and actions. . . . And as such it provides one of the essential dimensions for science, a uniform timeline within which things can be located and related and measured."[96] As Tom Wright says: "A truly first-century theological perspective would teach us to recognize that history, especially the history of first-century Judaism, is the sphere where we find, at work to judge and to save, the God who made the world."[97] The Jews and their Christian heirs believed that God was working out God's purposes in history, and so recognized the arrow of time with stark clarity. Specifically, for Christians, "the major steps of redemption culminating in Christ . . . in their uniqueness barred any possible flirtation with the idea of eternal and purposeless cosmic cycles."[98]

Historian of Science Allan Chapman has described the biblical emphasis on history. There are some aspects of the biblical story we would no longer see as events in time (such as an initiating creation at t = 0), but the overall perception of unique history is undeniable. The Bible's narrative

> brings a radical new concept into human thought: a historical timeline. Very different, in its exact chronology of events, to the cycles, circularities, ebbings and flowings of Egyptian, Babylonian, Far Eastern, and even Greek mythological and heroic (as opposed to philosophical) cultures. And I would argue that it was this very precise relationship between monotheism and a beginning, a

---

94. Hart, *Atheist Delusions*, 200.

95. Hart, *Atheist Delusions*, 201–2.

96. Turner, *Roots*, 70.

97. Wright, *Jesus and the Victory of God*, 662.

98. Jaki, quoted in Turner, *Roots*, 88.

sequence of events, and an ending which made a *scientific* view of the world possible.[99]

The historian of geology Martin Rudwick has stated that during the development of geological science "one major source—even arguably *the* major source—for this new vision of nature as historical was the strong sense of history embodied in the Judeo-Christian scriptures."[100] It is true that the proto-geologists acted on hypotheses that were superseded by discoveries about past ages (such as the idea that Noah's flood was the source of fossils), but most scientific hypotheses do not survive careful testing. The point is that their *historical mindset*, arising from their reading of the Bible, led them to formulate hypotheses connecting the present with the distant past, and so was vital for the development of geological thinking. When they first encountered fossils, their presumption of a continuous history enabled them to envisage sequences of natural events underlying the fossil record and the development of distinctive strata of rock.

Historian Tom Holland has supported Rudwick's contention. "The ambition of fathoming the deep past of the earth was one that had always come naturally to Christians." Holland cited Psalm 102:25-26 ("In the beginning you laid the foundations of the earth, and the heavens are the work of your hands"). He described the biblical vision of a world with its "beginning and a history, linear and irreversible." He reiterated that this understanding of time was distinct from the endless cycles assumed by most ancient cultures.[101]

We can never directly experience the past. It should be natural for Christians, whose lives are based on the non-repeatable histories of the prophets of Israel and of Jesus, and who diligently seek to understand those histories, to welcome and to find delight in the non-repeatable historical sciences such as cosmology, geology, and biological evolution.

99. Chapman, *Slaying the Dragons*, 239–40. Chapman does seem to differ from Jaki over whether Greek philosophical culture entertained cosmic cycles. Jaki insists that Plato and Aristotle adhered to the idea of never-ending cosmic returns. For example, Aristotle "subscribed to the universal validity and fundamental importance of cyclic returns . . . eternity and absolute necessity were for Aristotle two aspects of one underlying principle: the cyclic process." Jaki, *Science and Creation*, 111–12.

100. Rudwick, *Earth's Deep History*, 4.

101. Holland, *Dominion*, 436.

GOD IS TO BE WORSHIPED

The goodness of God and of creation induces worship. The Hebrew poets, sages, and prophets were exemplary founders of this tradition of worship which has endured in the Christian church.

> When I look at the sky which you have made,
> at the moon and the stars, which you set in their places—
> what are human beings, that you think of them;
> mere mortals, that you care for them?[102]

> How clearly the sky declares God's glory!
> How plainly it shows what he has done![103]

> LORD you have made so many things!
> How wisely you made them all!
> The earth is filled with your creatures.[104]

The Cavendish Laboratory in Cambridge has been the location of much revolutionary work in physics. A text was engraved over the door of the old Cavendish (in Latin; at the behest of the great physicist James Clerk Maxwell) and of the new (in Coverdale's English translation; at the suggestion of quantum physicist Andrew Briggs):[105]

> The works of the LORD are great
> sought out of all them that have pleasure therein.[106]

The early scientists (and their spiritual heirs) were impelled into their work by the same exuberant worship. Who could fail to value and study God's creation, given that it was seen as a sign of God's glory?

The astronomer Johannes Kepler prayed: "If I have been enticed into brashness by the wonderful beauty of thy works, or if I have loved my own glory among men, while advancing in work destined for thy glory, gently and mercifully pardon me: and finally, deign graciously to cause that these demonstrations may lead to thy glory and to the salvation of souls, and nowhere be an obstacle to that. Amen."[107] We may share his ecstatic

---

102. Ps 8:3–4.
103. Ps 19:1.
104. Ps 104:24.
105. Wagner and Briggs, *Penultimate Curiosity*, 439–40.
106. Ps 111:2.
107. Kepler, *Harmonice Mundi*, 1619; quoted by Gingerich, *God's Universe*, 112–13.

acknowledgment of God's glory as revealed in the cosmos: "Praise him, ye his celestial harmonies, and thou my soul, praise the Lord thy Creator, as long as I shall live, for both those things of which we are entirely ignorant and those of which we know only a little part, because there is still more beyond. Amen."[108]

Francis Bacon, who was an ardent popularizer of science, although not a scientist himself, promoted the development of science as a means of making known "the glory of God."[109] He prayed "May God, the Founder, Preserver, and Renewer of the Universe, in His love and compassion to men, protect the work both in its ascent to His glory and its descent to the good of Man, through His only Son, God-with-us."[110]

Galileo said that "the glory and the greatness of the supreme God are marvelously seen in all of His works and by divine grace are read in the open book of the heavens."[111] Galileo's praise is of particular note, as he is consistently depicted in the media as a lonely martyr for science, fighting against obscurantist religion. Media disinformation must not obscure the fact that Galileo was a devout Catholic Christian, and that his disagreement with other Christians was over the right way to interpret the Bible, and the validity of the prevailing Aristotelian cosmology.[112] As it happened, the Christian worldview of Galileo was to overthrow the pagan worldview of Aristotle. The so-called Galileo controversy led to the rejection of ancient Greek science and its replacement by the worldview arising from biblical thought.

And to pioneering chemist Robert Boyle, science (known in his day as *natural philosophy*) was "philosophical worship of God."[113] Boyle studied the "Booke of the Creatures" so that he could contribute to "the Glory of the Author of them."[114] His founding colleagues in the Royal Society provide abundant corroboration for the sincerity and depth of Boyle's worship.

108. Quoted by Gingerich, *God's Universe*, 121.

109. Wagner and Briggs, *Penultimate Curiosity*, 411.

110. Bacon, *Historia Naturalis*, 1622; quoted by Hooykaas, *Religion*, 71–72.

111. Quoted by Wagner and Briggs, *Penultimate Curiosity*, 195.

112. Brooke, *Science and Religion*, 101; McMullin, "Galileo," 56–57; Chapman, *Slaying the Dragons*, 106–7.

113. Quoted by Harrison, "Religion," 255–71.

114. Quoted by Wagner and Briggs, *Penultimate Curiosity*, 242.

3

SCIENCE AND THE NATURE OF HUMANITY

IN BIBLICAL FAITH, HUMANITY has been given a special status. Humanity is said to be created in the image of God,[1] the latter term often being given as its Latin form, the *imago Dei*. This was a strikingly novel claim. It would have shocked many people in the world of ancient Israel when they first heard it. In ancient pagan societies, only the king was considered to bear the image of God.[2] Denis Alexander has described how early pagan readers of Genesis 1 would have understood "image of God" terminology to mean that the kingly and priestly roles in society were allocated to the privileged few by a pantheon of gods. When they first encountered the idea that *humankind* was made in the image of God, they would have seen that this dignity was "now being delegated instead by the one creator God to the whole of humanity. In a stroke the entire ruling and priestly structure of Mesopotamian society was delegitimized. One type of creation order was to be subverted by another."[3]

The understanding that all humans bear the image of God refutes every kind of racial supremacy or elitism. It underlies concepts of human rights, so fundamental to a humane society and valued by humanists (secular or otherwise).[4] But it does not allow arrogant self-evaluations of humans as lords over creation. For the creature that bears God's image is made of the earth. What we possess is ours only as a generous gift. And to exercise

1. Gen 1:26–28.
2. Copan and Jacoby, *Origins*, 57.
3. Alexander, *Are We Slaves to Our Genes?* 199.
4. Hobson, *God Created Humanism*, 40, 130, 143; Spencer, *Evolution*, 74–75; Holland, *Dominion*, 400.

44

the powers of creatures that bear God's image is to act with the caring tenderness and love of God (see chapter 6).[5] To act as the image of God is to act on behalf of God.[6]

In its most basic sense, "image of God" terminology means that humans are commissioned to serve God on earth. We are God's representatives and are the recipients of God's address. This functional role thus implies a relatedness between God and humans and indicates that we have been endowed with something of the rationality of God. It follows that we can share some understanding of God's thoughts, and therefore of God's works. We are equipped to understand creation, that is, to do science.

To Galileo, mathematical properties are native to God's mind, and the human ability to do mathematics shows that "the human mind is a work of God and one of the most excellent."[7] Kepler also believed that geometry is a reflection of the mind of God, and that humans are enabled to share in his thoughts.[8] Similarly, William Whewell (the first systematic historian of science) noted "an affinity between the human and divine mind" in the human ability to "discover the laws of nature and express them mathematically."[9]

In our day the same sentiments can be found. For instance, Ernest Lucas has said: "Humans are made in the image of God. As a result we share something of the mind and wisdom of God and so can expect to have at least a limited understanding of the order of the cosmos which God designed." When we are engaging in scientific investigation, we can say with Kepler that we are thinking God's thoughts after him.[10] Similarly, Nick Spencer has written: "Nature was characterized by an order that was comprehensible to humans precisely because they were made in the image of its creator. The mind of God gave order to nature and as human minds reflected that mind, albeit imperfectly, they were in a unique position to detect nature's order."[11] To Harold Turner, "we ourselves as creatures also reflect our maker with minds that can work rationally and consistently and so be capable of understanding a universe structured in the same way."[12]

---

5. Bauckham, *Bible and Ecology*, 18.

6. Bauckham, *Bible and Ecology*, 30.

7. Quoted by Wagner and Briggs, *Penultimate Curiosity*, 191.

8. Wagner and Briggs, *Penultimate Curiosity*, 223, 227.

9. Brooke, *Science and Religion*, 19.

10. Lucas, *Science and the New Age Challenge*, 158; also 60–63.

11. Spencer, *Evolution*, 105–6.

12. Turner, *Roots*, 55.

The materialist must struggle to explain how neurochemical events in brain embody rationality; the Christian believes in rationality because it is possessed by God and devolved upon the *imago Dei*. The correspondence between the mind of God and the human mind underlies the capacity of the creature to apprehend something of the work of the creator[13]—that is, to think scientifically. The dignity we possess as creatures that can know something of God's thoughts has practical implications for the way we live and work and apply our intellects. Some of these will be considered below.

THE DIGNITY OF MANUAL WORK

Many Greek schools of thought denigrated manual labor. The idealistic philosophers of Athens considered that intellectual and spiritual development "could not take place in conjunction with manual work." To Plato, despite the importance of agriculture, the required manual work should be left to slaves. To Xenophon, a free citizen should not be involved in manual trades. To Aristotle, the free citizen should engage in contemplation and should not be involved in mechanical or mercantile occupations.[14] Greek philosophy thus entertained a tendency to see science as belonging to the head alone and not to the hands. The disregard of manual work was one factor that militated against their use of experiments.[15]

In contrast, the Jewish rabbis earned their own living as artisans, "with the ideal Israelite being a shepherd or devout peasant."[16] Amos was a shepherd; Jesus was a carpenter; Paul a tentmaker. "Those factors in Greek philosophy that hampered the development of experimental science are not present in the Bible."[17] Christian monasticism combined contemplation with practical technologies, as in agriculture, apiculture, animal husbandry, and building.[18]

As the scientific revolution approached, the "cooperation of artificers and scholars" led to the development of the experimental method. The new freedoms given to the artisan class, together with religious emancipation,

13. Thorson, "Spiritual dimensions," 250; Polkinghorne, *Science and Christian Belief*, 51.

14. Hooykaas, *Religion*, 76–78.

15. Hooykaas, *Religion*, 82.

16. Turner, *Roots*, 108.

17. Hooykaas, *Religion*, 84.

18. Turner, *Roots*, 110; Woods, *How the Catholic Church*, ch. 3.

led to the appreciation of every vocation as being divine.[19] People's day jobs were not simply a way of earning money for food; their work was itself a "divinely ordained activity." Indeed, the reformers insisted that all believers were priests, which meant that "all vocations were equally sacred."[20] Manual labor, like any occupation, was honorable so long as it was done for the glory of God.[21] Designing and performing experiments were not beneath the dignity of the scholar, nor were they demeaning to the saint.

THE END OF SLAVERY

Aristotle believed that a slave was an "animated tool."[22] And where slave labor was abundant, who needed instruments? David Hart suggests that "in a slave society, the aristocratic class remains insulated by its 'contemplative leisure' from practical knowledge, while those who are so debased as to work with their hands acquire a genuine consciousness of the intrinsic structure of concrete reality."[23] Slave cultures tended to segregate leisured thinkers and skilled tradesmen or artisans into separate cohorts of people. Brain and hand could come together only when the institution of slavery was rejected.

Biblical faith has often led the way in opposition to the institution of slavery. The recognition that people, regardless of status, are subject on the one basis to God's judgment and to God's offer of forgiveness must inevitably corrode the presumption that one man can own another. St. Paul, in his letter to Philemon, exposed the fallacy that a person could be both a slave and a brother or sister. Gregory of Nyssa, in 379 fulminated against the institution of slavery. "For any one at all . . . to assume mastery over another person is the grossest imaginable arrogance, a challenge to and a robbery of God, to whom alone all persons belong."[24] To Gregory, it was impossible that anyone could purchase the image of God. In Western Europe, the weakening of slavery may have contributed to the ascent of science from a "largely ineffectual realm of indolent aristocratic privilege to the realm of

19. Hooykaas, *Religion*, 92.

20. Harrison, *Bible*, 240.

21. Alexander, *Rebuilding the Matrix*, 93.

22. Hooykaas, *Religion*, 78; Hart, *Atheist Delusions*, 179.

23. Hart, *Atheist Delusions*, 73–74.

24. Hart, *Atheist Delusions*, 177–82; the quote is from p. 178.

material actuality."[25] It must be admitted, however, that Christians and their institutions were often very slow to see the implications of the gospel as far as the rejection of slavery was concerned.

CARING FOR THE NEEDY: MEDICINE

From the earliest times in Christian history, there has been an emphasis on the practical care of needy fellow human beings. This care would facilitate growth in proficiency of the healing arts. Jesus's parable of the good Samaritan[26] was of major significance, as it highlighted the place of mercy or compassion in relation to any neighbor in need.[27] The parable of the sheep and the goats[28] equated care for sick people with care for Jesus himself.

Christian philanthropy was based on *agape* love, a disposition that was lacking in paganism.[29] Christians developed the idea that they were *philoptochos*—friends of the poor—and believed that the poor were worthy of their care, and as recipients of their almsgiving. They were also committed to care for the dying—attitudes absent from much Greco-Roman paganism.[30] Christians believed (unlike the Greeks) in the possibility of healing. And they were committed to the desirability of working for human benefit.[31]

Christians motivated by the love of Jesus were instrumental in the development of hospitals and medical schools. Christianity was decriminalized at the start of the 300s. During that century, Basil founded his Basilica and hospital at Caesarea, which included facilities for travelers and the poor, for the aged, for lepers, and for accommodating physicians and nurses (AD 369). Ephrem set up a charity hospital of 300 beds in Edessa to address the effects of the plague (AD 375). He cared personally for his patients and he himself died from the plague.

In the West, Fabiola set up the first hospital in Rome (in the year 400). According to Jerome, she gathered the sick from the streets and cared for

25. Hart, *Atheist Delusions*, 74.
26. Luke 10:25–37.
27. Aitken et al., *Influence*, 7, Ferngren, *Medicine*, 104, 203–4.
28. Matt 25:31–46.
29. Ferngren, *Medicine*, 79, 86–88, 91–92.
30. Ferngren, *Medicine*, 88–89, 92.
31. Kaiser, *Creation and the History of Science*, 39–40.

the "wretched sufferers wasted with poverty and disease."[32] The monastery-associated hospital became a feature of Europe from thenceforth.

The practical mission of the early church, healing and helping, eventually "gave rise to the Christian traditions of medical science and technology in the middle ages."[33] In the early modern period, the liberation of theological thought further promoted medical knowledge by the rejection of ancient authorities (Aristotle, Galen) and by the promotion of the idea that all vocations, medical vocations included, were sacred.[34]

EDUCATION AND LITERACY

Biblical faith is, by definition, a commitment to a way of living that is based on the biblical narrative—especially the story of Jesus. As the first generation of Jesus-followers aged, the story they had been telling was written down for posterity. Like the Jews before them, the followers of Jesus intensely valued literacy—and this was true from the beginning of their movement. The teachers in the early church taught people to read, so they could reflect on the faith they were being taught. The culture of early Christianity was bookish.[35] Literacy is mind-expanding, a major prerequisite of scientific theorizing, data-gathering, analysis, and dissemination.

According to the New Testament scholar Larry Hurtado, "the activities of reading, writing, copying, and dissemination of texts had a major place—indeed, a prominence—in early Christianity that, except for ancient Jewish circles, was unusual for religious groups of the Roman era."[36] In Roman times, Jews and Christians read their texts in a way that was more akin to the practices of philosophers than of religious cults.[37] The four Gospels were highly distinctive for their times, being "substantial narratives of the one figure," and written within twenty years of each other.[38] The career of Jesus provoked an intense *bios*-writing activity. The use of lengthy letters as a "serious vehicle" for providing instruction (Paul, Ignatius) was

---

32. Aitken et al., *Influence*, 9–10.

33. Kaiser, *Creation and the History of Science*, 34–35.

34. Ferngren, *Medicine*, 141–42, 152.

35. Wright and Bird, *New Testament in Its World*, 849.

36. Hurtado, *Destroyer*, 105–6.

37. Hurtado, *Destroyer*, 110.

38. Hurtado, *Destroyer*, 123.

also a striking development in literary communication.[39] The early church was distinctive for the volume and diversity of its literary output, and for popularizing the codex (preferring the book form over the cumbersome scroll).[40]

Progress in piety is facilitated by knowledge of the scriptures. In the early church, the relationship between Christian theology and (pagan) philosophy had to be elucidated. For this reason, literacy was highly valued. Gregory of Nazianzus (329–89) argued that "the first of our advantages is education." He acknowledged that much pagan knowledge was incompatible with Christian faith but allowed that "from secular literature we have received principles of enquiry and speculation." He concluded that "we must not then dishonor education."[41] Gregory's attitude was typical of early church leaders.

The life of the scholar Boethius (477–524) was terminated prematurely—he was executed by a suspicious pagan king—but he established an approach to education that promoted, over many centuries, the survival of Western learning. This was despite the ever-present threats of starvation, plague, and invasion that prevailed through the harsh climatic conditions of the so-called Dark Ages. Boethius's younger contemporary Cassiodorus (c.490–585) assembled a famous library and assured his monks of the utility of secular knowledge for the understanding of Scripture. By this means he promoted an enduring love of learning in the monks of the Benedictine order.[42] Subsequently, the Celtic monastic tradition,[43] Bede (672–735; historian and acute observer of natural phenomena),[44] and Alcuin (735–804, architect of the Carolingian renaissance) sustained and advanced classical learning. Alcuin believed that "there was no improvement so radical that it might not be achieved by education."[45] He worked to make monasteries centers of literary excellence and to reform the clergy who had become carnal and ignorant.[46]

---

39. Hurtado, *Destroyer*, 121.

40. Hurtado, *Destroyer*, 128, 134–37.

41. Lindberg, "Science," 28–29.

42. Kaiser, *Creation and the History of Science*, 22–23.

43. For a somewhat racy account, see Cahill, *How the Irish Saved Civilization*.

44. McLeish, *Faith*, 47–49.

45. Holland, *Dominion*, 210.

46. Holland, *Dominion*, 211–12.

The church had a major role in the development of the universities.[47] It protected the well-being of students and supported the professors. It protected the liberty of the universities, fostered scholarly debate, and respected the autonomy of natural philosophy. Robert Grosseteste (d. 1253) in England (later Bishop of Lincoln)[48] and Albertus Magnus (d. 1280) in France[49] were outstanding figures in the development of the medieval university—and in generating momentum towards the growth of the scientific enterprise (about 30 percent of the curriculum of the medieval university was concerned with the natural world).

The development of the universities between 1200 and 1500 entailed that "hundreds of thousands of students—a quarter million in the German universities alone from 1350 on—were exposed to science in the Greco-Arabic tradition."[50] It is sometimes thought that the astronomer Copernicus was a lonely genius who appeared as if by magic. He was in fact the product of the centuries-long development of Christian universities, with their tradition of mathematics, astronomy, and the science of motion.[51] The thirst to understand cosmology, so manifest in Europe, was absent in cultures that differed in metaphysical outlook. As Tom Holland says, "The Christian inheritance of natural philosophy had revealed itself to be nothing if not Christian through and through."[52]

Luther was a contemporary of Copernicus, and he worked at the dawn of the so-called "scientific revolution." He believed that the progress of the gospel and the enrichment of civic life required that children receive a good education. Luther's letter *To the Councilmen of all Cities of Germany* (1524) "is still regarded as the original rationale for public primary and secondary schools wherever they are found. The arguments Luther generated in favor of public education for both boys and girls still lie at the base of all discussions of tax-supported education."[53]

47. Shank, "Myth 2," 19–27.

48. McLeish et al., "Medieval Multiverse," 161.

49. Woods, *How the Catholic Church*, ch. 4.

50. Shank, "Myth 2," 21.

51. Hart, *Atheist Delusions*, 58–61.

52. Holland, *Dominion*, 359.

53. Kittelson, *Luther*, 243–44.

THE SCIENCE OF BIBLICAL INTERPRETATION

Jews, Christians, and Muslims have been inveterate readers, motivated by commitments to their holy books. To Christians, the Bible speaks with authoritative power because it makes sense of so much history and experience. But it must be read intelligently, or people may end up misinterpreting it. Mis-readings have happened repeatedly in the past and, all too frequently, the results have been disastrous. It must follow that correct strategies of Bible reading are essential, and an enormous amount of effort has been expended in developing the science of interpretation (or hermeneutics). But the way people interpret *texts* affects the way they interpret *natural processes and events*. This section indicates how reading the book of *God's words* has shed light on reading the book of *God's works*. The metaphor of the two books was a major theme during the scientific revolution of the seventeenth century.

Rejection of ancient authorities

The Reformation democratized Bible reading. To Luther and other reformers, it was not sufficient to simply accept what church authorities said about the Bible. People had to read it for themselves and were responsible for how they applied and obeyed its message. This development in biblical hermeneutics effected a change in people's interpretation of the natural world. It was no longer acceptable to adhere to the pronouncements of the ancient philosophers, no matter how venerated they were. The science of Aristotle, Galen, or Ptolemy no longer compelled people's automatic assent. One was free—and indeed obligated—to investigate the natural world for oneself.[54] By the time of the Royal Society in the 1600s, it had become common practice to start a discussion by critiquing Aristotle and then proceeding to express and explore novel ideas.[55]

In order to practice genuine science, people must be free of the idols of "common opinion" and "official doctrine." People may indeed "respect human authority in church, state or science" but they must not let themselves be so deeply impressed by those authorities that they surrender their independence "because of the weight of the 'majority' or of 'tradition.'" Hooykaas said that "confidence in the possibilities of science and in the

54. Wagner and Briggs, *Penultimate Curiosity*, 220, 223.
55. Alexander, *Rebuilding the Matrix*, 98.

freedom of thought" are necessary consequences of authentic Christian faith.[56]

Interpreting scripture and natural objects

Reformation hermeneutics brought about a second paradigm shift in the way people approached nature. Until the sixteenth century, the Bible was subject to highly figurative readings. Texts were read at several levels, the most valued of which (the allegorical and anagogical) sought to look behind the surface meaning to higher "spiritual" meanings. In the same way, natural objects were perceived to be mere pointers to spiritual realities. But the reformers sought to simplify Bible reading. They rejected the unbridled and abstract speculation of anagogical interpretation and sought to understand the biblical text by engaging in more straightforward approaches. This had the flow-on effect of encouraging people to see natural phenomena not merely as symbols but as concrete entities in their own right. One could then study natural phenomena for what they were. An ant was not merely a metaphor of industrious labor; it was a social insect with a segmented body and an exoskeleton.

Peter Harrison has presented this perspective cogently. The Protestant reformers "insisted that the book of scripture be interpreted only in its literal, historical sense." This mentality "gave a determinate meaning to the text of scripture, and at the same time precluded the possibility of assigning meanings to natural objects." The new conception of nature arose because of "the collapse of the allegorical interpretation of texts."[57] It should be noted that "literal readings" do not imply a wooden rejection of all metaphor (as is often assumed today), but a careful attention to *authorial intent*.[58]

Using metaphors to reflect on the unpicturable

There may be a third way by which the reading of scripture has affected the approach to studying physical reality. Paganism represents spiritual beings and powers in terms of physical images. The use of idols effectively obliterates the difference between the divine and the created. But Israel

---

56. Quoted in MacKay, *Science and the Quest*, 40.

57. Harrison, *Bible*, 113; also Wagner and Briggs, *Penultimate Curiosity*, 231–32.

58. Harrison, *Bible*, 113.

was allowed no images of her God. The rejection of idols was one of the most fundamental stipulations of the law of Moses and the teachings of the prophets.[59] There were no physical props to imaging the divine. God was wholly "other" and could be described only by metaphors or models—God was a rock, fortress, lover, father, shepherd, king. The limitations of such metaphors were well recognized. God as *rock*, for instance, depicts only God's dependability as a foundation upon which we can build our lives.

The divine nature was known not from statues or carved images but from *God's actions in history*. The Jewish and Christian refusal to acknowledge the gods or to portray God as a physical image was radically distinctive. It is easy to forget how pagan Greeks and Romans recoiled from this repudiation of idols. They called Jews and Christians *atheists*.[60]

Perhaps the theological description of God in terms of metaphors and inferences from history prepared the mind for reflecting on physical realities that are not picturable. The nature of subatomic particles such as electrons cannot be specified in a simple, naïve, literalistic way. We may describe electrons metaphorically in terms of particles, waves, packets of energy, probabilistic clouds, even equations. The concept that two electrons continue to interact instantaneously even when separated by vast distances (entanglement)[61] confounds simple conceptualization. Quantum physics can "leapfrog" over an unknown (even unknowable?) physical reality to "arrive at a mathematically workable kind of knowledge."[62] Physicists are content to use abstract mathematics to depict realities that are not describable in any simple way. Polkinghorne has said that the quantum world is real but not naively picturable. "This gives physics a good deal in common with theology as the latter continues its search for an understanding of the Unpicturable."[63]

Even genes are abstractions. The "one gene, one protein" mantra with which I was introduced to biology fifty years ago has been well buried. Approximately 2 percent of the human genome embodies information needed to make proteins. A segment of such DNA can be copied to make one or

59. For example, Exod 20:4–5; Isa 44:9–20; 45:20—46:2; Mic 1:7.

60. Wright, *New Testament and the People of God*, 156; Hurtado, *Destroyer*, 38, 56, 184.

61. Steane, *Faithful to Science*, 77; Briggs et al., *It keeps Me Seeking*, 89–94; Wagner and Briggs, *Penultimate Curiosity*, 431–32.

62. Wagner and Briggs, *Penultimate Curiosity*, 399.

63. Polkinghorne, *One World*, 47.

many RNA molecules and one or a family of proteins. But such complexity is only the first step of the multi-layered versatility of genetic function. Over 70 percent of the genome is copied into RNA molecules—the majority of which do not carry information needed to synthesize proteins. What most of these long non-coding RNA molecules actually *do* is a mystery. Many RNA molecules are further processed into one or many little circles. Genes, and the RNA copies derived from them, are highly diverse in function, requiring a flexibility in the way we conceive of them.

Could the uniquely Jewish tradition of meditating on a God who could not be depicted as a familiar object facilitate the capacity to reflect on an unpicturable physical reality, and so underlie the disproportionately high contribution of Jews to science? Did their faith predispose them to reflecting on the unfamiliar, to "seeing" glimpses of the inconceivable? It seems likely that faith in a God who is wholly other would facilitate engagement with physical realities that are profoundly other.

Critical realism in theology and science

We approach scripture and the story of God's saving action in God's world in an attitude of humble confidence. *Humility* is required because we should always be aware that our objectivity is compromised, and our reasoning is limited. We often get things wrong. *Confidence* arises because we engage with an external reality that (given the wisdom and faithfulness of God) is constituted rationally and consistently. God is the guarantor of truth.

Tom Wright describes the appropriate way to read scripture as *critical realism*. This is "a way of describing the process of 'knowing' that acknowledges the *reality of the thing known, as something other than the knower* (hence 'realism'), while also fully acknowledging that the only access we have to this reality lies along the spiraling path of *appropriate dialogue or conversation between the knower and the thing known* (hence 'critical')."[64] In other words, critical realism issues from the understanding that knowledge is "part of the responsibility of those made in the image of the creator to act responsibly and wisely within the created world."[65]

The scientific way of thinking is also properly described as critical realism. Polkinghorne has described the two elements of the scientific mindset

---

64. Wright, *New Testament and the People of God*, 35; Wright and Bird, *New Testament in Its World*, 54–56 (italics in original).

65. Wright, *New Testament and the People of God*, 63.

in the following way. The *realism* element recognizes "that science actually does tell us about the physical world, even if it does not do so finally and exhaustively." The universe stands over against us. It has its own integrity. It is given. We seek to understand its inherent nature. On the other hand, the *critical* element "recognizes the subtlety and ultimate unspecifiability of the scientific method."[66] Our own rationality is not perfect. We need to test our hypotheses carefully, being prepared to discard (or at least modify) them. We must be sensitive to the inputs of our colleagues. Science gains, in other words, an ever-tightening grasp of an ever-elusive reality.[67]

We should neither sink into despair nor bask in arrogant self-confidence as we consider our aspirations to find truth. "For the scientist who believes in God . . . no matter how difficult he may find it to transcend the limits of his technique, no matter how plagued he may be by blind spots of knowledge or imagination, none of this denies that before him there stands a Judge of the truth and objectivity of any claim he makes."[68] We may be as cautious of our own capacities as we may be gladly confident of the truth that is upheld and known by God. Our knowledge of both theology and science develops by submitting our understanding of a mysterious reality to a reiterated process of testing and refinement.

66. Polkinghorne, *Beyond Science*, 18–19.
67. Polkinghorne, *One World*, 19, 22, 24.
68. MacKay, *Science and the Quest*, 54.

4

THE DEATH OF SCIENCE

IF IT IS TRUE that Christian presuppositions enabled the development of science, then we might expect that the loss of Christian influence would lead to the weakening and perhaps even the ultimate demise of science. In 1977, the chemist and philosopher Walter Thorson warned that "an age is passing . . . the age that is passing is the age of science."[1] This dire warning may seem implausible in our technology-besotted age, but we should differentiate between science (the quest to discover truth, with the intention of *understanding* nature) and technology (the utilitarian program to *control* and *profit from* nature).[2] It has been argued above that *science* operates on presuppositions stemming from the nature of God. *Technology* arises from an ingenuity and creativity that are typically human.

Thorson's solemn prognostication has been with me all my working life. It has informed me as science has increasingly come under pressure from a multiplicity of hostile streams of thought. Thorson gave several reasons for his somber warning.

THREATS TO SCIENCE

First, scientific knowledge has been conflated with the gain of power. Francis Bacon was the first to perceive that *knowledge is power*, and he saw this as *power to benefit humanity* ("the relief of man's estate").[3] Hooykaas in-

1. Thorson, "Spiritual Dimensions," 220.

2. Thorson, "Spiritual Dimensions," 221–22.

3. Hooykaas, *Religion*, 73; Russell, *Cross-Currents*, 72–73; Wagner and Briggs, *Penultimate Curiosity*, 250.

sisted that the "glory of God and the well-being of mankind ought to be our motives in extending our power over nature." He rejected the motivation of using science to enhance "personal power and money-making."[4]

But to Thorson, the contemporary relevance of the slogan "knowledge is power" is more sinister. Thorson noted that there has been a "fusion of science with technology," and this has changed the understanding of the power of science. "Having finally understood that scientific truth is a source of power, man has made the crucial decision that from now on the will to power and the uses of power should dictate the relevance and value of that truth."[5] In other words, the areas of scientific truth to be sought are those that give commercial, industrial, or even military advantages in a competitive world.

To C. S. Lewis, "Man's power over nature turns out to be a power exercised by some men over other men with Nature as its instrument. . . . Each new power won by man is a power over man as well."[6] Lewis had a reputation of being a bit suspicious of science, but in his concern over the misuses of scientific power, he may have been remarkably prescient. David Hart has warned that "Knowledge as power—unmoored from the rule of love or simply a discipline of prudent moral tentativeness—may be the final truth toward which a post-Christian culture necessarily gravitates."[7]

The trend is away from *pure science* towards research directed by economic pressure emanating from government and industry.[8] The motive for doing science is no longer truth for truth's sake; it is *utilitarian* in nature.[9] And the center of its utility is wealth generation. Forty years after Thorson delivered his pessimistic outlook, McLeish has lamented that scientists in the UK are required to specify the economic promise of their work.[10] Wagner and Briggs have cautioned that "the pursuit of national, corporate, and personal advantage have become much more visible drivers of scientific discovery"[11] relative to the motivations that inspired previous generations of investigators (the benefit of humanity and curiosity about the world).

4. Quoted in MacKay, *Science and the Quest*, 60.

5. Thorson, "Spiritual Dimensions," 221.

6. Quoted by Meilaender, *Bioethics*, 43.

7. Hart, *Atheist Delusions*, 233.

8. Thorson, "Spiritual Dimensions," 221.

9. Thorson, "Spiritual Dimensions," 221–22.

10. McLeish, *Faith*, 224.

11. Wagner and Briggs, *Penultimate Curiosity*, 411.

A consequence of the entrepreneurial take-over of science was said to be the prevalence of "short-term absurdly superficial yardsticks of achievement."[12] One must publish for funding, tenure, promotion, and prestige of self and institution. This puts pressure on scientists to get their work into press, even if work has not been replicated or publication is premature.

Second, Thorson cited the Age of Aquarius (aka the New Age movement) as a cultural stream that has profoundly subverted both Christianity and science. This was a loose movement of the 1960s–70s that was marked by several broad ideas. It was monistic (all individuality dissolves into an undifferentiated oneness), pantheistic (God *is* the cosmos and thus is to be found within us), relativistic (right is whatever feels right; all religions lead to the same divine reality or are true for those who believe them), and individualistic (life's goal is self-fulfillment).[13] A core attitude was the "devaluation of objective truth, the denial of its human relevance, and, ultimately, the denial of its reality."[14]

In this cultural stream (which has become deeply entrenched since Thorson wrote), feeling is valued above rationality.[15] Loss of recognition of divine authority leads to subjective existentialism—life's meaning is to be found in addressing one's own personal needs or wants. But in opposition to this prevalent mindset, Thorson insisted that science is not "cool"—it cannot be received by the mind "for which reality is only immediate, unplanned, and unreflected experience."[16] The Age of Aquarius is only one aspect of the pervasive postmodern worldview.[17] Harold Turner spoke of the severe threats to science coming from deep cultural levels, "from the current postmodern replacement of truth with cultural constructs."[18] He cautioned against the tendency to revert to tribal, re-divinized, animistic views of the universe.

---

12. Thorson, "Spiritual Dimensions," 222.

13. Lucas, *Science and the New Age Challenge*, 15–19.

14. Thorson, "Spiritual Dimensions," 222–23; quoting Francis Schaeffer with approval: "by denying the objective reality of God and the possibility of knowledge of Him, man has chosen a course which has also progressively emptied the natural world, and finally his own existence, of objective meaning."

15. Lucas, *Science and the New Age Challenge*, 29.

16. Thorson, "Spiritual Dimensions," 223–24.

17. Lucas, *Science and the New Age Challenge*, 149.

18. Turner, "Recasting," 172–73.

What then of those who assert that a particularly "European" or "Western" science has served the interests of colonialism and has disadvantaged indigenous peoples?[19] The word *science* needs to be used with particular care in this context. Science is the search to discover the nature of the universe and its component parts. By definition, it presupposes that there is one truth to be found, and so its findings are universally valid, regardless of people's tribal, linguistic, cultural, or religious backgrounds. It is true that many published scientific studies are highly provisional, irreproducible,[20] or otherwise erroneous, and that all human knowledge is ultimately provisional; but these limitations do not detract from the ideal that reliably validated findings are true for all of us.

The search to understand the nature of stars, atoms, earthquakes, or genes cannot be considered to be an instrument of oppression. However, scientific knowledge can be *exploited* for technological ends that are good or evil. Basic research into atoms can be directed into developing nuclear medicines, or nuclear bombs. When people speak (disapprovingly) of European *science*, they probably mean European *ideologies* that are often dressed up as science. Many *philosophical* ideas that are peculiar to (certain) European communities have indeed had devastating effects on colonized peoples and have had dehumanizing effects on all of humanity.

All of us, including tribal peoples, must distinguish between science and Western philosophical accretions to science. Ideological systems developed by Europeans include individualism, rationalism, scientism (the doctrine that only science discovers truth), evolutionism (the belief that biological evolution constitutes an entire worldview), eugenics and its close relative racism, materialism, the myth of economic expansionism ("neoliberalism"), industrialism, economism, consumerism, and nationalism. We could add colonialism.[21] These "-isms" have no necessary connection with science and are clearly inimical to the well-being of native peoples—and I should add, are hostile to the Way of Jesus.

The theologian Michael Northcott has described how Western businesses and governments have arranged for poor countries to repay debts by the "clear-cutting of ancient forests and the environmental exclusion" of

19. For a debate occurring in New Zealand: Young, "Why Punish a Scientist"; Ross, "New Zealand Academics."

20. Editorial, "Replicating Scientific Results," 359–60.

21. Colonialism is not limited to Europeans. Throughout history, powerful empires, nations, and tribes have sought to subjugate and exploit those who are more vulnerable.

peasant farmers and tribal peoples from their ancestral lands.[22] We should rejoice in science but reject the idolatrous and parasitic "-isms" extrapolated from it. Māori and other indigenous peoples are right to protest against Western materialist ideologies but are wrong if they consider such pseudo-scientific ideologies to be *science*.

The particularities of the European Enlightenment—a philosophical, not a scientific movement—attempted to "emancipate" Western thinking from "Christian and other religious dogma." The Enlightenment was built on the belief that humans are separate from nature, and it disdained the indigenous inhabitants of tropical ecosystems, and their very local ways of "knowing, using, and living in these landscapes."[23] Such Enlightenment thinking has often led to the expulsion of indigenous populations from land designated as natural reserves. Not only is this immoral; it is misguided, as the "future health and biodiversity of protected landscapes globally may be contingent on Indigenous occupancy, use, and stewardship."[24] Western Enlightenment thought is parasitic upon science, as depicted in Fig. 3.

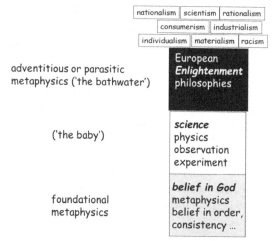

Fig. 3. Western philosophies and science
Enlightenment philosophies are parasitic upon science and must be distinguished from it.
This diagram is an elaboration of Fig. 1. We must not throw out the baby (science) with the
bathwater (philosophies or ideologies that are parasitic upon science).

22. Northcott, "Ecology and Christian Ethics," 225.

23. Fletcher et al., "Indigenous Knowledge," 2.

24. Fletcher et al., "Indigenous Knowledge," 3.

We should note that what has been described as the *science* of indigenous or tribal peoples is not science but accumulated cultural wisdom. Such practical expertise does not represent a quest to *understand* the world but to *live wisely within it*. For example, Polynesians are rightly revered for their navigation skills, having sailed the vast Pacific to populate virtually every habitable island situated therein. This life-preserving skill is not science, however, because the Polynesians would have achieved their stupendous maritime feats of discovery irrespective of whether they considered the stars to be gods or sites of thermonuclear fusion. The traditions of Māori and other indigenous peoples may provide a rich source of information on groundwater flows or changes in ocean currents. Such traditions may be appropriated with great benefit in ecological studies.[25] But the value of such ancient insights does not make them science.

Other extraordinary tribal skills have enabled Australian aboriginals to survive in the water-stressed outback, and of Inuit to survive in the icy Arctic (environments in which Europeans died in droves). The effect of removing Aboriginal peoples (who wisely managed the outback for millennia) from the western deserts of Australia (in the 1960s) "was catastrophic, resulting in uncontrolled wildfires and a degradation of the ecological qualities of the land."[26] The amazing folk wisdom of the Inuit has been described by Canadian scholars, who state that

> In even the simplest foraging societies, people depend on a vast array of tools, detailed bodies of local knowledge, and complex social arrangements and often do not understand why these tools, beliefs, and behaviors are adaptive. We owe our success to our uniquely developed ability to learn from others. This capacity enables humans to gradually accumulate information across generations and develop well-adapted tools, beliefs, and practices that are too complex for any single individual to invent during their lifetime.[27]

The indigenous people of the Amazon and South-East Asian rainforests have domesticated important crops, promoted biodiversity, maintained forest structure and resilience, and contributed to the preservation of diverse ecosystem services. Removal or marginalization of indigenous people

25. Crow, "Māori Meeting House," 228; Sidik, "Weaving Indigenous Knowledge," 285–87.

26. Fletcher et al., "Indigenous Knowledge," 4.

27. Boyd et al., "Cultural Niche," 10918–25.

has degraded the ecological quality and resilience of these long-peopled landscapes. There is an urgent need "to embrace situated Indigenous and local knowledge systems." This can "provide new insights into understanding how biodiverse environments have been used and managed sustainably well before the so-called Enlightenment."[28]

When studying theology, I came across the Xhosa saying *umuntu ngumuntu ngabantu* ("a person becomes a person through persons"). This emphasizes the priority of the community over the individual. We become human only because we are nurtured by those who were human before us. Our humanity is not genetically encoded but is dependent on relationship—in the first instance with those who were persons before us, and ultimately with God.[29] It is a deeply biblical insight and urgently needs wider currency—and is incompatible with Western individualism.

It follows that people in New Zealand should learn both from science and from the accumulated cultural wisdom of the Polynesians. The former would be taught in physics, chemistry, and biology classes (for example) and the latter would have input into how scientific knowledge is applied.[30] Māori perspectives should rightly inform the uses of scientific knowledge, although should be subject to the same careful evaluation as any other form of knowledge. In fact, Western Christians should consider it an urgent priority to see how certain Māori perspectives should bring them back to a more authentic biblical faith. But indigenous wisdom is not science.

Third, Thorson noted a resurgence of superstition and magic. His concern is that "Magic is pure technique, divorced from reason. Its concern is with power and the will to power, not with reflective understanding of an objective, faithfully consistent reality."[31]

Of significance, thirty years after Thorson aired his concerns, David Hart has commented on the reappearance of magical thinking. In the ancient world, magic was seen as "a kind of terrestrial technology concerned with impersonal cosmic forces." Christian thought rejected the magical pagan worldview. The world was seen to be governed by God. Its workings were rationally ordered. There were no extra-physical forces that could be

---

28. Fletcher et al., "Indigenous Knowledge," 5.

29. Finlay, *Evolution and Eschatology*, ch. 3.

30. If Polynesians sought to compare their evolved technologies with those of Europeans, apposite topics might include the Stonehenge-building Neolithic people, the seafaring Vikings, and the road-building Romans.

31. Thorson, "Spiritual Dimensions," 225.

controlled by human skill—whether by prescribed words or ritual actions. But now, quite apart from astrology and similar New Age ideas, science is itself treated as magic. People think that "because we *can* do something, we *should* do it"—without any qualms as to whether there are overarching considerations of wisdom and morality that should temper their actions.[32]

Fourth, popular culture has often adopted a philosophy of pure existentialism. Nothing deserves commitment except the feeling of the moment. The mindset of existentialism rejects in principle intellectual or spiritual authority.[33] And Thorson wrote before the age of reality television, celebrity culture, mobile phones, social media, and the metaverse. Thorson offered his observation that in the West, most good science students come from a tradition that accepts personal discipline, moral responsibility, and commitment to the objectivity of moral truth and goodness. He explicitly located these in Judaism and Christianity.[34]

SIGNS OF DECAY

Thorson concluded with the observation that "the cultural forces and ideas which threaten the survival of science are precisely the same forces and ideas which are opposed to Christianity and the biblical ideas of God, man and the world. . . . If the age of science comes to an end, it will really be because people collectively have not cherished and sustained that practicing faith in the reality and authority of truth."[35] Through my working life, many of Thorson's concerns seem to have been realized. Appropriately forewarned, I have been able to understand the growing threats to science in deeply theological terms.

Science has been captivated and perverted by materialistic ideologies in the past. Disastrous episodes have included the development of eugenics (fathered by the brilliant Francis Galton, d. 1911) and the Marxist perversion of plant genetic science (the brainchild of Trofim Lysenko, who influenced Soviet agriculture through the mid-twentieth century). Millions of people have suffered, either because they were deemed to be of inferior genetic stock (eugenics) or because they starved (Lysenkoism).

32. Hart, *Atheist Delusions*, 233.
33. Thorson, "Spiritual Dimensions," 228.
34. Thorson, "Spiritual Dimensions," 229–30.
35. Thorson, "Spiritual Dimensions," 231.

There have been sustained attacks on science by powerful capitalistic commercial interests, of which the tobacco and fossil fuels industries take pride of place. These axes of evil have orchestrated disinformation campaigns in order to deny the tobacco-cancer connection and the contribution of anthropogenic CO_2 to climate change. They have used the same tactics, organizations, and in many cases the same personnel in their efforts to discredit science. They have even recruited scientists as their propagandists. They have campaigned to undermine confidence in evidence. They have sown doubt on the validity of well-established findings and of the scientific method itself.[36]

Doubt or uncertainty is integral to science, operating as it does at the limits of human knowledge. However, the tobacco industry pioneered the tactic of misapplying scientific tentativeness to well-supported facts. Tobacco industry insiders knew as early as did academic scientists (early 1950s) that their product caused cancer. They could identify dozens of carcinogens in cigarette smoke—but vigorously denied the cancer danger for decades.[37] A tobacco industry memo (1969) stated that "Doubt is our product since it is the best means of competing with the 'body of fact' that exists in the minds of the general public."[38] When scientific evidence demonstrated persuasively that second-hand tobacco smoke caused cancer (and other diseases) the tobacco industry set out to tarnish that evidence. In fact, repeatedly, industries protecting their harmful products have labelled inconvenient but rigorous science as "junk."[39] Another way of undermining science was to create the impression that a scientific consensus was faulty and that the issue under consideration was still "controversial." The mantra, cynically developed, was "Maintain the controversy."[40] Between 1992 and 1994, most articles (62 percent) in newspapers and magazines that discussed the link between second-hand tobacco smoke and cancer described it as being "controversial," even though the scientific evidence

36. McCarthy, "Climate Science," 34–52; Keane, "How the Oil Industry"; Supran, "Fueling," 702.

37. Proctor, "History," 87–91.

38. Oreskes and Conway, *Merchants*, 34.

39. Oreskes and Conway, *Merchants*, 136; for the repeated use of the "junk science" strategy, see also 143, 163, 223, 232, 236.

40. Oreskes and Conway, *Merchants*, 140, 241.

of its harm was conclusive (and was recognized as such, privately, by the tobacco industry).[41]

The campaigners who set out to discredit climate science asserted that scientists and science journals were part of a conspiracy to misrepresent the truth.[42] Journalists were pressured to give purveyors of doubt and reputable scientists equal status and equal exposure in the media. Equal exposure was proclaimed as "balance'"—even though a supposedly balanced presentation of pseudoscience and the scientific consensus constituted information bias in favor of the former.[43] The media were complicit in perpetuating the "balance" between climate-change denialism and reputable science.[44] Denialists wrote to directly mold public opinion and they eschewed peer review by qualified scholars.[45] Underlying the attack on climate science was the mantra that "technology will save us."[46]

But the tobacco and fossil fuels industries are not alone: special interest groups have sought to undermine science pertaining to environmental hazards such as lead, radioactive radon gas, asbestos risk, pesticides, acid rain, and ozone-destroying chemicals.[47] Likewise, a small coterie of scientists opposed the consensus that "Star Wars" technologies could not provide security against nuclear attack. Part of this strategy was to rubbish the idea of the "nuclear winter," and to portray opposing scientists as ideologically motivated.[48] More recently, society has been presented with COVID-19 denial coupled to the anti-vaccination movement, and the proliferation of conspiracy theories, which are impervious to any form of evidence raised against their claims.[49] There is increasing disquiet at the resultant threats and invective that are directed towards scientists and physicians who have made public statements pertaining to the COVID-19 pandemic.[50]

Truth has been a victim of the "evolution wars" waged between certain Christians and atheists such as Richard Dawkins. These highly polarized

41. Oreskes and Conway, *Merchants*, 242.

42. Oreskes and Conway, *Merchants*, 211–12.

43. Oreskes and Conway, *Merchants*, 214–15.

44. Oreskes and Conway, *Merchants*, 241–42.

45. Oreskes and Conway, *Merchants*, 269–70.

46. Oreskes and Conway, *Merchants*, 182–83, 255–57.

47. Oreskes and Conway, *Merchants*, 6, 144.

48. Oreskes and Conway, *Merchants*, ch. 2.

49. Hotez, "Anti-Science," e3001068.

50. Editorial, "COVID Scientists," 236; Nogrady, "Scientists," 250–53.

combatants share the belief that physical and biological processes (such as evolution) are necessarily alternatives to the biblical concept of divine creation, and they read the Bible without careful attention to genre. To such Christians, one can only say that evolution (say of humans from primate progenitors) has compelling evidential support,[51] that the Genesis creation accounts are artfully composed stories that present Israel's God in lustrous contrast to pagan deities,[52] and that the biblical concept of creation must encompass every conceivable natural process.[53]

To Dawkins and his ilk, one can only say that the misrepresentation of theology-science relations as inherently conflicted can only embitter lay-people towards science. For example, in 1860 there was a debate between Bishop Wilberforce and T. H. Huxley ("Darwin's bulldog") over Darwin's new book, *Origins*. Dawkins has memorialized this event by erecting a plaque at the venue in Oxford. But Dawkins's triumphalistic account is pure legend. There is no contemporary account of what was said, no critic's review identifying the winner, and no evidence that the event was of any significance in the acceptance of Darwin's evolutionary paradigm.[54]

Peter Harrison has expressed concern at the "flight from science." He has lamented that "science is no longer underpinned by a shared set of moral values," as it was during its emergence in the seventeenth century, when it received its justification from Christian theology. Harrison cites self-appointed apologists for science who do more harm than good. These include Francis Crick (who asserted that personal identity is no more than neurons and molecules) and the cosmologist Stephen Weinberg ("the more the universe is comprehensible, the more it also seems pointless"). Similarly, Gingerich cites biologist William Provine, who makes the wild and unwarranted leap from evolutionary biology to the metaphysical (religious) dogma that there is no ultimate meaning in life.[55]

Such nihilistic materialism will lead many to reject science. But Harrison rightly insists that the sciences are not the bearers of meaning and

51. Finlay, *Human Evolution*.

52. Copan and Jacoby, *Origins*, 32–42.

53. Polkinghorne, *Science and Christian Belief*, ch. 4 esp. 73–76; Finlay, *Evolution and Eschatology*, 23–25.

54. Chapman, *Slaying the Dragons*, 113–20; Dixon, *Science and Religion*, 73–76; Livingstone, "Myth 17," 152–60; Brooke, *Science and Religion*, 40–42.

55. Gingerich, *God's Universe*, 74; Gingerich also chides G. G. Simpson (who conflated biology with purposelessness) and Jerry Coyne (who conflated evolution and atheism) for confusing science with their own personal metaphysics: *God's Planet*, 98–101.

value—and never will be, and that "scientistic excess needs to be limited by an appropriate modesty."[56] People of course are free to adopt a scientistic metaphysics. But to pretend that scientism is justified by science is yet another instance of category error, arising from confusion or even duplicity (as discussed, chapter 1).

Fabricated controversies such as the tobacco-cancer link, climate change, and the evolution wars have undermined science and have left large segments of the population confused. It may be that this confusion—even cynicism—extends to medicine, the media (which prefers confrontation and scandal to nuanced truth), and politics. To the pioneers of science—the natural philosophers of the 1600s—God was the guarantor of truth (chapter 2). If standards of truth are ailing in our increasingly post-Christian, postmodern world, the remedy is not to place our hope in science, but to return to the God upon whose truth science is most securely founded.

Science is increasingly distanced from its biblical roots. Is it a coincidence that there is an epidemic of fabricated data in the scientific literature? Bogus research articles, potentially numbering in the thousands, have been produced to order by "paper mills." Grossly fraudulent publications are concentrated in molecular biology,[57] but they are also found in computer science[58] and even in clinical trials reports.[59] Interestingly, an ideological system (Marxist materialism), that seems to provide a permissive environment for such duplicity, is that which most vociferously insists on the supremacy of science over "religion," and which has been remarkably slow in disciplining people who generate inauthentic research publications.[60]

We are not suggesting that fraudulent behavior in science is the norm. The great majority of scientists are horrified at any whiff of duplicitous practice. But the insidious problem of fraudulent "science" emphasizes that the ongoing vitality of science is totally dependent on a high standard of integrity that transcends science itself. Science is not the bedrock of truth. Rather, Truth is the bedrock of science. We would do well to reflect on the source of that Truth.

---

56. Harrison, "Science, Religion, and Modernity"; see also Polkinghorne, *Beyond Science*, 124.

57. Chawla, "Single 'Paper Mill,'" doi:10.1126/science.abb4930; Shen, "Seeing Double," 132–36; Else and Van Noorden, "Fight," 516–19; Van Noorden, "Journals," 14–15.

58. Van Noorden, "Hundreds," 160–61; Else, "Tortured Phrases," 328–29.

59. Bero, "Stamp Out Fake Clinical Data," 167.

60. Else, "China's Clampdown," 19–20.

5

DISCOVERY IN THEOLOGY
AND SCIENCE: SURPRISE

I SUSPECT THAT ONE of the main reasons people do science is that when researchers stumble upon some new aspect of reality, they experience a sense of exhilaration, a thrill of wonder. I write *stumble* because many transformative discoveries were not expected by those who made them. As Paul Helm stated, "in the history of human enquiry the facts have time and again turned out to be surprising. Who would have thought, at one time, that the earth was round, that heavier-than-air machines could be made to fly, or that a vitamin C deficiency causes [scurvy]?"[1] The late Judah Folkman, cancer researcher extraordinaire, stated that none of his several paradigm-changing discoveries was ever anticipated in his applications for research funding.[2] His transformative discoveries were all, shall we say, fortuitous.

When scientists find something new, it is often unanticipated, astonishing, or counter-intuitive. A new understanding may even be (according to physicists) frankly weird if not "spooky." The discovery takes everyone by surprise.[3] And onlookers are often incredulous—they may refuse to believe new ideas that challenge common sense or that contravene old ideas held for generations. Common sense is not a good guide as to what we might learn of the physical world.

1. Helm, "Why Be Objective?" 35.
2. Plenary lecture, AACR Conference, Houston, 1984.
3. Polkinghorne, *One World*, 50.

The events underlying Christian faith have the same capacity to catch people by surprise. We encounter a reality that is not of our making—that is too outlandish to have been concocted by a scriptwriter—and that has a compelling power of its own. We feel that we have made a discovery about some aspect of reality that is independent of us—that is *given*—and that makes satisfying sense of many aspects of our lives or of history. Common sense is not a good guide as to what we might learn of God and God's ways.

SURPRISES IN ISRAEL'S HISTORY

The story of ancient Israel repeatedly describes events and ideas that are unprecedented, unanticipated, and indeed remote from what people might expect. It is astonishing that in a world of polytheistic superpowers, a few people in the tiny confederation of Israelite tribes proclaimed and celebrated a creator God of love, faithfulness, and peerless authority. The appearance of Israelite faith in the one good God represents an island of lustrous monotheistic belief in a vast sea of brooding polytheism. In the first eleven chapters of Genesis, the Israelites repurposed the stories of the ancient Near East to proclaim the uniqueness and holiness of Israel's God. All of these eleven chapters critiqued ancient culture and beliefs.[4] This novel faith must have come as a colossal shock to the Canaanites and Babylonians—and anyone else who came across Israel's subversive ideas. (It also provided an understanding of reality that was uniquely conducive to the pursuit of science, as noted above.)

But the nation of Israel came to a sickening end. Babylon crushed Israel and its monarchy, razed Jerusalem and destroyed its temple in 587 BC. Many of the ablest people were taken into exile. All the signs pointed to the conclusion that Babylon had extinguished Israel's story and its aspirations as well. But following that disaster, Israel's prophets uttered new expressions of the incomparable glory of Israel's God. Israel's "conquest in the early sixth century BC should, by any logic, have been its end. The fact that it wasn't is noteworthy. The fact that it resulted in the universal vision of [Isaiah chapters 40–66] is remarkable."[5]

The new interpretation of Israel's journey with God arose in the context of exile, when (it seemed) the gods of Babylon had utterly vanquished the God of Israel. That such disaster issued in a new confidence seems

4. Copan and Jacoby, *Origins*, 25.

5. Spencer and White, *Christianity*, 109.

incongruous, inexplicable, incredible. Indeed, Jaki said that the resurgence of Jewish monotheism in exile "constitutes a most baffling chapter in cultural history," and that the prophets' ridicule of Babylonian idolatry is without parallel "in any other ancient literature, religious or philosophical."[6] Similarly, George Knight wrote that the prophets' "interpretation is so strange, so utterly different from the thoughts of any other human being at any time in history, that the reader is compelled to ask whether it does not actually come from the mind of God."[7]

Knight wrote of the paradox that it was only when the Jewish people were dead and buried that this revelation of their redeeming God could take place.[8] Jewish and—ultimately—Christian faith were conceived in the context of crushing defeat and oppression. The Jewish and Christian stories were written from the anguished underside of history.

SURPRISES IN THE HISTORY OF JESUS

The events that gave rise to Christian faith were also met with surprise and incomprehension by most people who came across them. Tom Wright has emphasized how the whole career of Jesus was seen by his contemporaries as strange, shocking, paradoxical. And yet the teaching and life of Jesus cohered in a way that made sense. "Happy are you poor" (or you who hunger, or weep or are persecuted).[9] Jesus's response to the petty power-plays of his disciples was, "If one of you wants to be great, you must be the servant of the rest."[10] He told them that the greatest one must be like the youngest—the person of least status; the leader like the servant.[11] "I your Lord and Teacher have just washed your feet"[12]—an astonishing inversion of social convention. To encounter Jesus necessarily challenges our pre-conceptions and leads us to discover realities of which we could not have dreamt. We are surprised by truth.

Many Jews of Jesus's time struggled under an intolerable burden of oppression. They yearned for the time when God would set them free; when

6. Jaki, *Science and Creation*, 143–44.

7. Knight, *I AM*, 4.

8. Knight, *I AM*, 10.

9. Luke 6:20–26; Matt 5:3–13.

10. Mark 10:43.

11. Luke 22:26.

12. John 13:14.

God's kingdom would come. Jesus announced the inauguration of the kingdom of God. Jesus's preaching placed him firmly in the context of early first-century history and thought. But Jesus announced a *kind* of kingdom that confounded the expectations of his disciples and of other listeners. They "don't understand what's going on, and they fail to pick up the significance of his strange stories and powerful deeds." Indeed: "*Part of the meaning of the kingdom, in the four gospels, is precisely the fact that it bursts upon Jesus's first followers as something so shocking as to be incomprehensible.*"[13]

The way Jesus claimed the right to forgive sins was *startling* and indeed *shocking* to his contemporaries. He circumvented the authorized channels involving the temple and the priests.[14] Jesus called people to follow him as the true *but surprising* fulfilment of Israel's story. He was bringing about the long-anticipated great restoration of Israel, the return from exile, in a way that people *were not expecting.*[15] First-century Jews were hoping for a messiah who was a national liberator, a military genius. But Jesus turned this expectation on its head. "Jesus' redefined notion of messiahship . . . pointed to a fulfilment of Israel's destiny which *no one had imagined or suspected.*"[16]

The most inexplicable part of Jesus's proclamation was that his life's work would culminate in a violent death. This prospect was something "for which his first followers were *completely unprepared* and that, indeed, they refuse at first to countenance."[17] Jesus saw "a *strange* vocation for himself, to take upon himself the suffering predicted for the people."[18] Jesus's *strange,* subversive announcement was that God was at last becoming king through Jesus's own life and death—a death that would have a *shocking* interpretation.[19] Jesus provided that interpretation when he made it clear that his own suffering was an integral "part of the *strange* process whereby the kingdom finally dawns."[20]

We follow Jesus's journey to the unimaginable climax of his career. Jesus said that he would be "lifted up."[21] This term is ambiguous; and it

13. Wright, *How God Became King*, 197. The italics are Wright's.

14. Wright, *Jesus and the Victory of God*, 435.

15. Wright, *Jesus and the Victory of God*, 473.

16. Wright, *Jesus and the Victory of God*, 539. Italics mine.

17. Wright, *How God Became King*, 198.

18. Wright, *Jesus and the Victory of God*, 573.

19. Wright, *Jesus and the Victory of God*, 466.

20. Wright, *Jesus and the Victory of God*, 601.

21. John 3:14; 12:32.

could be taken to allude to both crucifixion (the ultimate humiliation) and coronation (the ultimate exaltation). Inconceivably, both meanings were to be true! Wright points to the paradox that *lifting up* refers to both cross and kingdom.[22] John the Gospel-writer surely intended this profoundly paradoxical juxtaposition of opposing ideas. The time of Jesus's crucifixion was the time of Jesus's coronation. A scandal of miscarried justice and subsequent maximally degrading execution was the way in which the rule of the creator God would be established.

The corrupt chief priest, Caiaphas, saw Jesus as a menace to the *status quo*, and in fact to national security. He stated that it was better that one man should die for the people, instead of having the whole nation destroyed.[23] He wanted to eliminate Jesus and spoke from the perspective of a conniving, self-serving politician. But John intended his readers to understand Caiaphas's phrase in a way that Caiaphas could never have suspected. The statement anticipated Jesus's redeeming death on behalf of Israel, and indeed of humanity. Jesus would indeed die to save all the people.

When Caiaphas posed the question of Jesus: "You are the Messiah, the Son of the Blessed God?"[24] he sought to entice Jesus into incriminating himself. To Caiaphas, the idea that Jesus might be the Messiah was preposterous. But Caiaphas's words could be understood equally as a statement: "You are the Messiah, the Son of the Blessed God!" How we understand those words depends entirely on the inflection of the spoken voice.[25] And Mark intended the irony. Despite Caiaphas's hostility to Jesus, he had unwittingly—and contrary to his intentions—confessed Jesus's divine appointment as Savior of Israel! This was Caiaphas's unintended "confession of faith!"[26]

The narrative proceeds to the ironies of Jesus's trial before Pilate, the Roman governor.[27] Pilate's (deeply ironic) interrogation is on the nature of Jesus's kingship.[28]

---

22. Wright, *How God Became King*, 231.

23. John 11:51–53.

24. Mark 14:61.

25. Wright, *Jesus and the Victory of God*, 523.

26. Wright, *How God Became King*, 237–38.

27. John 18:28—19:16, GNT.

28. Wright, *How God Became King*, 144–47.

Pilate: Are you the King of the Jews?

Jesus: My kingdom does not belong to this world, . . . if my kingdom belonged to this world, my followers would fight . . . .

Pilate: Are you a king, then?

Jesus: You say that I am a king. I was born and came into the world for this one purpose, to speak about the truth.

Pilate: And what is truth? . . . Remember, I have the authority to set you free and also to have you crucified.

Jesus: You have authority over me only because it was given to you by God.

For Pilate, the dialogue was hopelessly opaque. His wholly conventional understanding of *king, kingdom,* and *authority* could find no traction with Jesus's radical redefinition of the terms. This exchange truly represents the clash of two incommensurable paradigms. Jesus's unheard-of style of kingship repudiates the world's paradigms of royal (and secular) authority. His way of being king is one of weakness, not of naked power; of peace, not of violence. It is characterized by truth, not duplicity. Its authority of submission is exercised over that brutally imposed by Rome (and the myriad autocracies before and after Rome). Hart sees the trial of Jesus as the great watershed of history. Jesus exchanged the "form of God" for the "form of a slave."[29]

> The new world we see being brought into being in the Gospels is one in which the whole grand cosmic architecture of prerogative, power, and eminence had been shaken and even superseded by a new, positively "anarchic" order: an order, that is, in which we see the glory of God revealed in a crucified slave, and in which (consequently) we are enjoined to see the forsaken of the earth as the very children of heaven.[30]

This other-worldly story is the unique alternative for everyone who grieves over the unbroken human quest to subjugate others.

The irony of this situation is exposed in Pilate's final exchange with the Chief Priests.[31]

---

29. Hart, *Atheist Delusions,* 171; quoting the hymn of Phil 2:5–11.

30. Hart, *Atheist Delusions,* 174.

31. John 19:15–16.

Pilate: Do you want me to crucify your king?

Chief Priests: The only king we have is the Emperor.

In the past, Jewish freedom-fighters, in ferocious combat with pagan (Greek) powers, had famously said "We have no king but God." In their idealism, they would not compromise with pagan rule. The chief priests, in confessing that they had no king but Caesar, had now repudiated the long-held hope of Israel. They had rejected Jesus, and so had rejected their true king.[32]

Jesus was ridiculed as king by Roman soldiers (complete with a crown of thorns and royal robes)[33] and by the Jewish authorities.[34] Their motivation was purely mockery. But the Gospel writers intended us, their readers, to perceive what Jesus's opponents could never have imagined. This was the time when Jesus was being crowned king. It was the moment when God's kingdom was (at last!) inaugurated, the climax of Israel's tumultuous history. The promise of new creation was now being realized.

The *titulus* (official statement of guilt) on Jesus's cross read "This is Jesus the king of the Jews."[35] In all probability, Pilate intended this as an insult to offend the Jewish leaders.[36] Pilate knew that Jesus's kingship was of a different order from any he had ever encountered before. But to the Gospel writers, the *titulus* documented the time in history when Jesus was invested as God's chosen king.[37]

As Jesus had moved towards his destiny in Jerusalem, he had been approached by two ambitious disciples, James and John, who asked whether they could sit on his right and his left when Jesus became king.[38] Jesus replied that these places were not his to give. The Gospel writers indicate that when Jesus was crucified, the places on his right and left were occupied by two criminals[39]—indicating that *this* was the time when he came as king, the time of his coronation.

---

32. Wright, *How God Became King*, 146.

33. Mark 15:16–20; John 19:1–3; Wright, *How God Became King*, 230.

34. Mark 15:31–32.

35. Mark 15:26; John 19:19.

36. Wright and Bird, *New Testament in Its World*, 246–47.

37. Wright, *How God Became King*, 218–19.

38. Mark 10:34–40.

39. Mark 15:27; Wright, *How God Became King*, 227.

The climax of Mark's Gospel occurs at the moment of Jesus's death, when the presiding Roman officer exclaimed, "This man was really the Son of God!"[40] Mark and the pagan soldier would have understood the phrase "Son of God" in widely different ways. But to Mark, Jesus was exalted as God's Savior of the world only at the moment when, abandoned by God and humanity, his bloodied carcass hung limp on a Roman gibbet.[41]

Wright describes the previously unimaginable denouement of Israel's history as "the death of the strange non-Messianic Messiah."[42] In this astonishing paradox, the first disciples and indeed all of humanity catch an arresting glimpse of God's counter-intuitive workings. God acts, not in brutal coercive power, as is the time-honored norm of human beings, but in self-giving love. God in Jesus became the Suffering Servant, "the total opposite of the gods and heroes" imagined by human beings.[43] It is discovery, an encounter with a reality that we could never have anticipated. It is a haunting challenge to the data of our experience and addresses our anguished questions about suffering and hope.

About twenty years after Jesus's death, St. Paul emphasized the sheer strangeness of the story he taught:

> As for us, we proclaim the crucified Christ, a message that is offensive to the Jews and nonsense to the gentiles; but for those whom God has called, both Jews and gentiles, this message is Christ, who is the power of God and the wisdom of God. For what seems to be God's foolishness is wiser than human wisdom, and what seems to be God's weakness is stronger than human strength.[44]

St. Paul discovered—despite every long-held presupposition, and against all expectation—that when Jesus died, he had inaugurated God's kingdom. Paul described this in the apparently oxymoronic phrase *Christos estauromenos*—the Messiah crucified.[45] Jesus as crucified Messiah was *scandalous* to Jews, *incomprehensible* to gentiles.[46] The climax of Jesus's life was unimaginable, sheer bewilderment, to those who expected a traditional sort

40. Mark 15:39.

41. Knight, *I AM*, 65.

42. Wright, *Jesus and the Victory of God*, 574.

43. Knight, *I AM*, 72.

44. 1 Cor 1:23–25.

45. Wright, *How God Became King*, 237.

46. Wright, *Jesus and the Victory of God*, 487; Instone-Brewer, *Jesus Scandals*, 76–80.

of liberator—a militant who would vanquish foreign armies. No one could have concocted this story. A divine reality has burst in on us.

It goes without saying that the direct sequel to Jesus's crucifixion, his resurrection, was totally unanticipated by gentiles ("resurrection could not happen") and Jews ("resurrection would happen only at the end of time"). Tom Wright says of the pagan world of the first century: "death was all-powerful. One could neither escape it in the first place, nor break its power once it had come. The ancient world was thus divided into those who said that resurrection couldn't happen, though they might have wanted it to, and those who said they didn't want it to happen, knowing that it couldn't anyway."[47]

As far as the Jewish world was concerned, ideas of resurrection were widespread but variable and vague. "But nobody imagined that any individuals had already been raised or would be raised in advance of the great last day."[48] In contrast, the reality of the bodily resurrection of Jesus, however surprising and counter-intuitive it may be, remains the sober claim of every person who, in the first century, staked his or her life on following the Way of Jesus.

The gospel (or good news) proclaimed by the church impacted society by its blinding originality. A convicted Jew, crucified, resurrected, and sharing in the very identity of the deity, was the very savior for which humanity had yearned. To Greeks and Romans, heroes and emperors just might be divinized—but certainly not a crucified outcast representing the lowest of humanity's flotsam. As Holland has said, the idea that "a man who had himself been crucified might be hailed as a god could not help but be seen by people everywhere across the Roman world as scandalous, obscene, grotesque." And this sense of disgust would be felt most keenly by Jews. "No more shocking a reversal of their most devoutly held assumptions could possibly have been imagined. Not merely blasphemy, it was madness."[49] This radically new evaluation of humanness underlay the tenets of the Christian revolution: that all people have rights, no matter how poor or marginalized they might be. All are born equal. All deserve food, shelter and freedom from persecution. These ideas are not self-evident. They were conceived in the particularity of Judeo-Christian history.[50]

---

47. Wright, *Resurrection*, 82; Wright and Bird, *New Testament in Its World*, 277.

48. Wright, *Resurrection*, 205; Wright and Bird, *New Testament in Its World*, 293.

49. Holland, *Dominion*, 6.

50. Holland, *Dominion*, 540–41.

The basis of Christian faith takes us unawares. It is surprising but compelling, satisfying. We do not invent it—we discover it. John Polkinghorne has said that "The doctrines of a tripersonal God and of his making himself known in human terms, have about them those elements of surprise and intellectual profundity which are characteristic of the best scientific theory."[51] The amazement that accompanies our engagement with the histories of Israel and of Jesus is like that which is experienced in the discoveries of science.

SURPRISES IN COSMOLOGY

Copernican astronomy provides an example of how new ideas have been rejected in favor of traditionally received wisdom. Copernicus argued that the earth moves around the sun, rather than the sun (and the other heavenly bodies) moving around the earth, as Ptolemy had proposed. Copernicus's ideas were accepted only gradually, but not because people were obscurantist. Rather, "in the sixteenth century, fixing the sun at the center and throwing the earth into dizzying motion seemed completely ludicrous, a violation of common sense."[52] Surely (people thought) if the earth was really spinning, people would be thrown into space. And it would be harder to walk west than to walk east. Copernicus's idea appeared to be totally ridiculous![53]

Two generations after Copernicus, the great Danish astronomer Tycho Brahe still could not envisage how the Earth, a "lazy sluggish body," could undergo motion as swift as the stars themselves.[54] People did not reject Copernicus's heliocentrism because they were willfully, perversely ignorant. They rejected Copernicus's proposal because it seemed to be totally at odds with the world they knew. It took time before people could accommodate the strange new astronomy into their world picture.

We live with the reigning Big Bang cosmology. What could be more counter-intuitive than the notion that the universe once fitted into a volume smaller than an atom? But this crazy idea seems to be the unavoidable conclusion of the observation that the galaxies are flying away from each other. (Follow the galaxies back in time, and they fly towards each other.)

51. Polkinghorne, *Reason and Reality*, 98.

52. Gingerich, *God's Universe*, 17, 90–95.

53. Gingerich, *God's Planet*, 12.

54. Gingerich, *God's Planet*, 24.

Big Bang physics also accounts for the relative abundances of hydrogen and helium in the universe: these elements were formed in the primeval explosive event.

A third line of evidence for Big Bang cosmology is the cosmic microwave radiation that pervades the universe, and that is leftover energy from the Big Bang. This radiation was discovered by accident. Robert Wilson and Arno Penzias were using a receiver dish to study microwave radiation but found that they picked up (what they considered to be) random noise. They tried many ways to eliminate this static—even cleaning out their antenna on the hypothesis that the static came from pigeon droppings—before the realization dawned that this signal represented the all-pervading radiation that arose at the Big Bang.

SURPRISES IN ATOMIC AND QUANTUM PHYSICS

In the early 1900s, Ernest Rutherford discovered (unexpectedly) that most of the mass of atoms was present in dense points of matter, now called nuclei. He bombarded very thin gold foil with alpha particles, expecting that all of the latter would simply pass through the foil. The conventional wisdom was that mass was evenly distributed in atoms. But to his astonishment, some of the alpha particles rebounded from the foil—they had impacted points of mass that would be known as *nuclei*. Rutherford said that his initial observation was as surprising as if a 15-inch artillery shell had bounced back when fired at a piece of tissue paper.[55]

Research into the very small has led to the "strange counter-intuitive subatomic world of quantum theory." This reality is "totally unpicturable for us, but it is not totally unintelligible."[56] Niels Bohr, one of the pioneers of subatomic research, stated that anyone who is not shocked by quantum theory has not understood it.[57] We are told that "an electron can be in more than one place at the same time . . . experiment and theory both showed that an electron could spread itself out as it travelled though tiny gaps, forming a sort of blurry electron-smudge, which then reassembled to a particle at

---

55. Polkinghorne, *Beyond Science*, 10; Hutchings and McLeish, *Let There Be Science*, 67–68.

56. Polkinghorne, *Beyond Science*, 79.

57. Wilkinson, *God, the Big Bang and Stephen Hawking*, 56.

the end of its journey." The world that quantum physics presents to us is "unrecognisable."[58]

The element carbon is a necessary component of complex biological molecules. Carbon needs to be abundant for life to occur (and indeed is the fourth most abundant element in the universe). The carbon nucleus is generated in stellar furnaces. Fred Hoyle wondered how carbon is formed in abundance in stars. He speculated that when two small nuclei (helium, beryllium) combine to form a carbon nucleus, the contributed energies *precisely* add up to an energy content at which the new carbon nucleus is stable. If another helium nucleus then bombards a carbon nucleus, the combined energy is not quite right to satisfy the requirements for a stable oxygen nucleus, so oxygen is generated only inefficiently, and carbon accumulates. Hoyle's proposal was called "outrageous." When his prediction was tested experimentally and shown to be correct, he himself was astonished at the result. He was an atheist but stated that "some superintellect has monkeyed with physics."[59]

SURPRISES IN MEDICINE AND BIOLOGY

Discoveries of biologists too have been accompanied by moments of either amazement or outright incredulity. In the mid-1800s, the physician Ignaz Semmelweis was deeply concerned at the high rates of mothers' deaths from sepsis following delivery of their babies. This carnage occurred in wards overseen by physicians and their students, who also examined cadavers, but not in wards under the care of midwives. In 1847, Semmelweis demonstrated that thorough handwashing by physicians could prevent transmission of infections to mothers. When handwashing was introduced as routine practice in his post-natal ward, death rates dropped sharply. Nevertheless, the medical establishment did not believe his results, and ridiculed him. (Bacteria had not been discovered at that stage, and Semmelweis could only hypothesize the existence of "cadaverous particles.") When Semmelweis remonstrated strongly in support of his finding, he was placed into a mental asylum, in which he was assaulted and died. The cruel injustice of this story is outrageous to us—but may have been less so if we had lived in an age when invisible infections agents were as yet unknown.[60]

58. Hutchings and McLeish, *Let There Be Science*, 72.

59. Gingerich, *God's Planet*, 121–27.

60. Stang et al., "Twenty First Century," 437–445.

In 1911, a young virologist called Peyton Rous was studying a type of cancer (a sarcoma) that occurred frequently in flocks of chickens. He discovered that if cancers were homogenized, and the gloop passed through a very fine filter, the cell-free filtrate could cause cancers when injected into other chickens. Infectious cancers? Transmitted by some unbelievably tiny agent? His superiors were not impressed with Rous's work and moved him on to another project. Rous did not know it at the time, but he had discovered an oncogenic virus (now known as Rous Sarcoma Virus) and had pioneered work that led to the field of cancer genetics. His story finishes more happily than that of Semmelweis, as he lived to see his ideas vindicated. He was awarded the Nobel Prize for Medicine in 1966, at the age of eighty-seven.[61]

It had long been considered that chronic stomach inflammation (gastritis), underlying the development of gastric ulcers and stomach cancers, was the result of stress or excessive acid production. In the early 1980s, Barry Marshall and Robin Warren demonstrated that a bacterium, *Helicobacter pylori*, induced gastritis, which often presaged the development of serious stomach disease. Gastroenterologists were initially hostile to the idea that a spectrum of stomach diseases was caused by a bacterial infection, and that those diseases could be prevented by something as simple as the use of antibiotics. Marshall persisted in arguing his case, and eventually *H. pylori* was accepted as a major player in the development of the range of gastritis-associated diseases. In due time (2005) Marshall and Warren also received the Nobel Prize.[62]

The revolution in molecular biology occurred following the discovery of the structure of DNA, the molecule of heredity. DNA was known to be composed of long chains of alternating sugar (deoxyribose) and phosphate units. DNA also included four heterocyclic bases: adenine (A), cytosine (C), guanine (G), and thymine (T). James Watson (a microbiologist) and Francis Crick (a physicist) wondered how the bases were arranged with respect to the sugar-phosphate strands. Their "experimental work" was limited to playing with cut-out models of the bases. One day in 1953, in a sudden moment of totally unexpected illumination, Watson perceived that A fitted snugly with T, and C with G, and that these paired bases would lie in the center of a helix formed by two intertwined sugar-phosphate

---

61. Kumar and Murphy, "Francis Peyton Rous," 660–63; Weiss and Vogt, "100 Years," 2351–55.

62. Hellstrom, "This Year's Nobel Prize," 3126–27.

chains. These non-chemists had stumbled onto the double-helical structure of DNA, and with it, they had discovered the physical basis of heredity: how information could be embodied in DNA, how it could be transmitted faithfully between generations of organisms, and how it could be altered when mutations arose. A flash of intuition had capped off a large amount of patient experimental work by many other investigators.[63]

The human genome project was undertaken to discover the order of the three billion bases in the genome. A first draft was published in 2001. Again, there were major surprises: "the most shocking outcome"[64] was the discovery that the human genome possesses about twenty-one thousand genes, about the same number as is found in the worm *Caenorhabditis elegans* used in labs for genetic studies. *C. elegans* is about one millimeter long. Surely humans are more complicated than minute worms! Latest data support the twenty-one thousand number for human protein-coding genes. Human genes must be more versatile functionally than those in worms. In addition, the human genome possesses a similar number of nonprotein-coding genes.[65] The roles of most of these are not known, but it is likely that they contribute to our complexity in ways that we cannot at this time anticipate.

Most of my research history has been in the rather mundane field of anti-cancer drug development. But even in my work, there have been moments of incredulity when experiments generated unexpected—indeed seemingly inexplicable—results. The laboratory in which I worked was seeking to develop cytotoxic (cell-killing) anticancer drugs. One way to assess the effects of such drugs is to expose cancer cells to a drug for a brief time (conventionally, one hour), remove the drug, and culture the cells to see how many had retained the ability to grow into a visible mass of cells (a colony). Clearly, as drug concentrations increased, cell killing would also increase, and fewer cells would generate colonies.

However, one day I was given a locally synthesized experimental drug to test. I chose a range of drug concentrations that I anticipated would cover a suitable range of cytotoxic effects. But to my astonishment, as the concentration of this poison *increased*, the number of cells that were killed *decreased*. More poison, less killing! I needed several experiments to convince myself that the results were real (Fig. 4).[66] We eventually decided that

63. Portin, "Birth," 293–302.

64. Gingerich, *God's Planet*, 82.

65. Willyard, "New Human Gene," 354–55.

66. Finlay and Baguley, "Selectivity," 271–77.

this surprising behavior arose from the ability of the drug to *poison* its target enzyme at low concentrations (which killed cells) but *inhibit* the enzyme at higher concentrations (which turned off the cytotoxic pathway).[67] For the curious, the U-shaped killing curve represented the way our drug perturbed the interaction of the enzyme topoisomerase-2 with DNA.

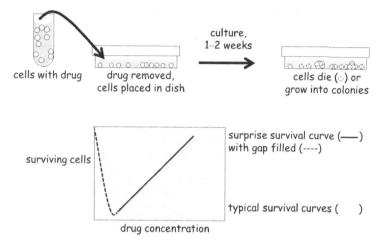

Fig. 4. An unbelievable experimental result

Scheme, above: how anticancer drugs are tested. Cancer cells are treated with drug and cultured to see how many can still multiply. In this illustration, ten cells are cultured and two (20%) form large colonies.

Graph, below: typical survival curves (thin grey lines); initial result showing increased survival with increased drug concentration (thick line); and later results showing decreased survival using lower drug concentrations which killed cells effectively (dotted line).

We were presented with similar counter-intuitive results with an unrelated drug called paclitaxel (used clinically to treat breast cancers). As a laboratory tool, this drug is conventionally used in cell cultures at a relatively high concentration to stop cells from dividing—but it does not kill them immediately. However, a research student found that if the concentration was *decreased* by fifteen-fold the drug became acutely cytotoxic. It was a great surprise to find that low concentrations of paclitaxel cause cells to rapidly disintegrate whereas much higher concentrations generate cells that can no longer divide, but which remain intact and metabolically viable, at least for several days.[68]

67. Baguley et al., "DNA-Binding," 552.

68. D'Mello, "Role," 118.

A third example will suffice to illustrate how we do not *create* patterns in nature, but we *meet them as given*. A scientist in our laboratory set out to characterize a selection of proteins made by cells derived from melanomas (aggressive skin cancers) from a cohort of patients. We would regularly meet and discuss her results but could detect no consistent patterns. Eventually we decided we had to publish her data with the rather minimalistic message that there was no significant relationship between the set of proteins made and patients' melanoma cell populations. We wrote an article describing our results, but a reviewer asked for more incisive analysis.

So we had another look at our old data. At this late stage, we suddenly—and unexpectedly—perceived that the melanoma cells fell into two groups, as defined by the proteins they made. We did not contrive the results to fit in with some cherished theory. The patterns in the data were there all along, unrecognized, until they took us by surprise in a flash of illumination.[69] Our hypothesis arising from this work is that melanoma cells are specialized for one of two behavior types: they may concentrate either on *survival* (making them resistant to therapy) or on *invasion* (enabling them to spread and destroy adjacent tissue).

A SUMMARY

To return to Polkinghorne. Theological proposals (such as the duality of divine and human natures in Christ) and scientific ideas (such as the persisting influence between quantum mechanical entities after they have interacted) are counter-intuitive, but they are grounded in experience. "They are not flights of ungrounded speculation. . . . That is the basis of the comradeship of theology and natural science." Oddness is a sign of the way things are.[70] Christian theology and science share an amazing feature. The insights they provide are often surprising. Their content is not *invented* but *discovered*. To peruse the data of history (on which Christian faith is based) and of science is to be amazed by findings that are unexpected but coherent. There are real worlds "out there" that are not of our fabrication, and we are taken aback—and delighted—whenever we gain a new glimpse of how those worlds are constituted.

There is corollary of this sense of discovery. There is a vast amount of truth that we have not yet stumbled on. The Christian theologian and the

69. Kim et al., "Heterogeneity," 97.

70. Polkinghorne, *Science and Creation*, 92–93.

scientist should be deeply humble people. Our knowledge is desperately partial.[71] We should not be embarrassed by our own ignorance. Nor should our ignorance be an excuse for rejecting ideas that we find unpalatable. What little we know, of the mind of the creator or of the nature of the creation, is a wonderful gift, to be received with gratitude and a sense of awe.

It has been said that people cannot seriously consider foundational beliefs of Christian faith now that we are in the scientific age or living in the twenty-first century. Colin Russell observes that there have been "attempts to evacuate the Christian faith of its essential content, so as not to offend the susceptibilities of 'scientific man.'" In the light of our experiences of surprise, such pronouncements are "not only misguided but leave most scientists profoundly unimpressed."[72] We dare not limit theological understanding by what we consider to be conceivable in a scientific age. Polkinghorne considers such an attitude to be unscientific. Experience, not "reason" should set the agenda.[73]

We cannot deduce what God or nature is like by starting with self-evident axioms, which can never take account of the surprising nature of reality. The character of God cannot be inferred from science, for all the prestige it has gained by its new understandings of the physical world. We go from beliefs about God to the mindset or worldview that enables us to practice science (chapter 2); but we may go only very cautiously, and only part of the way, from scientific results to beliefs about God. True, for those who believe (for other reasons) in God, the order and profoundly personal nature of our world are consistent with the reality of such a personal creator. But science presupposes the nature of God; it cannot discover or analyze God.

Sir James Jeans suggested that science can point only to God as the Great Mathematician.[74] Another astronomer, Owen Gingerich, has said: "There just isn't a bullet-proof deductive argument for the existence of God from the evidences of physics. And even if there were, would it be more than a god of large numbers?"[75]

Donald MacKay said, "I think that people attempting to use scientific data to make a proof for the existence of God, . . . apart for Biblical

71. 1 Cor 13:12.

72. Russell, *Cross-Currents*, 225.

73. Polkinghorne, *One World*, 83.

74. Houghton, *Search for God*, 44.

75. Gingerich, "What Does Physics," 98.

revelation about Him, are backing a loser."[76] A contemporary of MacKay, the pioneering X-ray astronomer Robert Boyd, stated that "the God in whom the Christian believes is not the Object of propositions that one can set about proving or disproving, but the Subject of encounter, an encounter centered on our moral response to Christ."[77] Likewise, John Polkinghorne has said that a study of the cosmos can lead us no further than to the Cosmic Architect. "The God and Father of our Lord Jesus Christ is to be sought by other means."[78] The 3Ps concur, stating that we cannot argue our way from science to a faith in God.[79] For, as Homes Rolston points out, God is not merely the Benevolent Architect; God is rather the Suffering Redeemer.[80]

The scientist and the theologian each share a sense of encounter with a mysterious but exhilarating reality. But we cannot deduce a way to God. Philosophy or physics are simply inappropriate approaches to knowing God.[81] We discover that the way to God is through Jesus—surprising though that may seem. We cannot predict what science will divulge. But there is a real world out there. It is an interactive duality of the spiritual and the physical. As noted (chapter 2), that understanding is the gift of ancient Hebrew thought to science.

The early church leader Tertullian (d. 220) stated with characteristic vehemence, "[The Son of God] was buried, and rose again: it is certain because it is impossible." This was no retreat from rationality, but a celebration of the counter-cultural and counter-intuitive nature of the gospel.[82] He could have been referring equally ("certain because impossible") to many discoveries of science. Such a mind-set does not, of course, justify the credulous acceptance of any rumor or conspiracy theory. It does require that reliable data, no matter how unexpected or shocking, should be subject to thoughtful and ultimately consensual interpretation that fulfils the criteria of elegance, coherence, economy, and fruitfulness.

76. MacKay, *Science and the Quest*, 64.

77. Boyd, "Reason," 122.

78. Polkinghorne, *Science and Creation*, 86.

79. Briggs et al., *It Keeps Me Seeking*, 169.

80. Quoted in Bimson, "Considering," 79.

81. Worthing, *God, Creation, and Contemporary Physics*; Lewis and Barnes, *Fortunate Universe*.

82. McGrath, *Dawkins' God*, 99–101.

6

SCIENCE AND THEOLOGY
IN SUSTAINABILITY AND JUSTICE

THE DIALOGUE BETWEEN SCIENCE and Christian theology must continue. Our lives depend on it. Science tells us that human activities are placing huge strains on the ecosphere. Pollution, resource depletion, deforestation and erosion, extinction of species and climate change are issues of continual concern and increasing urgency. Despite much talk and hand-wringing, most indicators describing the health of the biosphere are heading in the wrong direction. Transformative change is required.[1]

This chapter features the ecological reflections of a secular scientist, the Canadian ecological economist Bill Rees, and a theologian, Michael Northcott. I have found Rees's writings to be illuminating and compelling. He has described scientific aspects of human overexploitation of nature impactfully. But he is not confident of the ability of the human organism to take appropriate remedial action. Northcott takes us further into deep-seated moral principles, such as justice, that are set into creation and which we ignore at our peril.

ECOLOGICAL FOOTPRINTS: ECOLOGY AND ECONOMY

We need to be aware of the demands that we place on our planet. Two ecological economists, William Rees and Mathis Wackernagel, have developed a method of comparing what Earth produces with what we humans appropriate for our own use. What Earth produces is its *biocapacity*. What

1. Diaz, "Pervasive," eaax3100.

humans consume is our *ecological footprint*. These two quantities can be weighed against each other at the scales of humanity-at-large, of nations, of communities, or of individuals.

The ecosystem services that Earth provides, biocapacity, includes both *products* that we need (such as food, water, fiber, wood) and *processes* that break down, recycle, or absorb our wastes. Multiple other ecosystem services—from mineral cycles and erosion control to pollination and pest control—are vital to our well-being but will not feature in what follows.

Our consumption of biocapacity, or footprint, reflects the question, "How much of the biologically productive capacity of the planet is being used to power the human enterprise?"[2] People's footprints are the sum of all they consume and the ecological systems that they need to process their waste. Waste removal is a component of our footprint because it draws on nature.[3]

Biocapacity and footprint are compared using a single metric: a *standardized area* of Earth's surface that indicates both productive capacity and consumption. The unit used in each case is *global hectares per person* (g ha per person). This is calculated from five types of productive area: cropland, grazing land, fisheries area, forestry land (which provides timber *and* sequesters carbon dioxide, CO_2), and built-up (urban) land (Fig. 5). People's footprints are defined as "the aggregate area of land and water ecosystems required by specified human populations to produce the ecosystems goods and services they consume and to assimilate their carbon wastes."[4]

---

2. Wackernagel and Beyers, *Ecological Footprint*, 10.

3. Wackernagel and Beyers, *Ecological Footprint*, 17.

4. Rees and Wackernagel, "Shoe Fits," 1001701.

Fig. 5. Our ecological footprint
How much of the Earth's productive surface (cropping, grazing, forestry, fisheries, and
urban) is used to support my lifestyle, or that of my community?

A waste product of particular concern is CO_2, a greenhouse gas (GHG). CO_2 is produced when fuels (especially non-renewable fossil fuels—natural gas, oil, coal) are burnt, and is accumulating in the atmosphere. It is the most rapidly growing component of our ecological footprint and the major cause of climate change. Fifty percent of the fossil fuel ever used has been consumed in the last twenty-five to thirty years—that is, half the fossil fuel-derived CO_2 ever emitted has been released only since the early 1990s. This profligate energy use is highly anomalous in 200,000 years of human history.[5]

The methodology of eco-footprint analysis has been criticized. It is unable to account for declines in the health of productive areas on Earth. It cannot take account of the loss of soil, or of groundwater resources, or of fisheries, or of biodiversity. And the size of the carbon footprint depends on the assumed rate at which forests sequester carbon.[6]

However, both those that criticize eco-footprint analysis,[7] and those that promote it,[8] agree that it is conservative in its estimation of the damage that humans have been inflicting on ecological systems. We cannot dismiss its findings as exaggerations. We should take the implications of

5. Rees, "End Game," 138.

6. Blomqvist et al., "Does the Shoe Fit?" e1001700.

7. Blomqvist et al., "Does the Shoe Fit?" e1001700.

8. Rees, "Eco-Footprint Analysis," 371; Rees and Wackernagel, "Shoe Fits," e1001701.

footprint analysis very seriously. There are, of course, areas of uncertainty. There are different ways of defining footprints. But the message is clear: our current ecological footprints are unsustainable.[9]

Comparing global biocapacity and ecological footprint

At present, the *biocapacity* of Earth is 1.63 g ha per capita. This is the total productive area of Earth divided by the total human population of the planet. As indicated above, this means that for each human being, on average, 1.63 ha of productive Earth area *are available* to support his or her lifestyle. (This does not take into account the needs of wild animals, which also have legitimate requirements for space and food.)

For humanity as a whole, the average global *ecological footprint* is 2.75 g ha per capita. This indicates that each person *uses* 2.75 ha to support his or her lifestyle. At this point we encounter a seeming anomaly. Consumption exceeds production, and it does so (currently) by a factor of 1.69:

$$\frac{\text{global ecological footprint}}{\text{global biocapacity}} = \frac{2.75 \text{ g ha/person}}{1.63 \text{ g ha/person}} = 1.69$$

A footprint that exceeds biocapacity seems nonsensical. How do we account for the implication that we consume more than is available?

Multiple Earth lifestyles (overshoot) and ecological debt (unsustainability)

Any ratio of footprint to biocapacity that exceeds a value of 1.00 should concern us. A ratio of 1.69 is alarming, because it indicates that human consumption exceeds the productivity of the biosphere. We are effectively using the productivity of 1.69 planet Earths. We are in *ecological overshoot*, a state that was first seen in ~1970 and that has increased in magnitude in each subsequent year. Rees reported humanity's ecological overshoot as 40 percent (in 2002), as 50 percent (in 2008), as 68 percent (in 2016) and as 73

---

9. Hoekstra and Wiedmann, "Humanity's Unsustainable," 1114–17.

percent (in 2021).[10] Rees describes overshoot as the meta-problem, to which all other ecological challenges, climate change included, are contributors.[11]

We are not only fully using what ecosystem services produce but are consuming the systems that provide them. We are living not only on the interest but on the capital. Living in overshoot is possible only by drawing down non-renewable stocks.[12] A population can remain in overshoot only by depleting vital ecosystems and non-renewable resources.[13] Another way of expressing overshoot is to indicate that humanity is accumulating *ecological debt*. This situation cannot continue forever. It is *unsustainable*. Paying back our debt (that is, allowing depleted ecosystems to recover) may take more time than was needed to degrade them. It may not even be achievable in the case of severely degraded ecological systems.[14]

The warning is stark. Rees wrote in 2002 that to ensure the long-term integrity of the ecosphere, "an absolute reduction (by as much as 50%) in the total dissipative load[15] imposed on ecosystems by people may be required. This increases to a reduction of at least 80% in high-income countries in order to create the ecological space needed for necessary growth in the developing world."[16]

Variation in ecological footprints

Footprint analysis of individual countries provides more disquieting insights. Ecological footprints vary widely by country. People in rich countries consume much more than those in poor countries. Table 1 provides representative footprint values.[17] Countries vary by up to twenty-fold in their footprints. Earth's bounty is being shared very unequally.

10. Rees, "Ecological Economics Perspective," 40; Rees and Wackernagel, "Shoe Fits," 1; Rees, "Avoiding Collapse," 3; Rees, "Plague Phase," 7; Rees, "Growth through Contraction," 104.

11. Rees,, "Growth through Contraction," 99.

12. Rees, "Ecological Economics Perspective," 40; Rees, "Globalization," 262; Kitzes et al., "Shrink and Share," 467–75.

13. Rees, "Globalization," 263.

14. Kitzes et al., "Shrink and Share," 471–72.

15. "Dissipative load" is the transformation of useful energy and biomass into unusable waste.

16. Rees, "Ecological Economics Perspective," 41.

17. World Population review. "Ecological Footprint by Country"; another dataset is presented graphically in Wackernagel and Beyers, *Ecological Footprint*, 18–25.

For any country, the ratio of its footprint to global biocapacity indicates the number of planet Earths that would be needed to support humanity if everyone on Earth had the level of consumption of the people of that country. The richest countries have a five-Earth consumption footprint. The poorest have a 0.3- to 0.4-Earth footprint (Table 1). New Zealand has a footprint of 5.6 g ha per person, similar to those in most European countries. If everyone in the world had a Kiwi-sized footprint, humanity would require 5.6/1.63 = 3.4 planet Earths to support the population. That means, humanity would require *at least two more planet Earths* to support its Kiwi-level lifestyle. But extra Earths are not to be found.

Another way of visualizing this data is to indicate the date by which a country uses up its annual allocation of Earth's harvest. This date is that country's *overshoot* day. The richest countries have claimed their year's allocation by March; the poorest countries keep well within their annual budget of ecosphere products (Table 1, right column). In 2021 overshoot day occurred on 29 July, after which humanity maintained itself and its manufactured capital assets, and expanded the economy, by further eroding remaining stocks of natural capital (fisheries, forests, arable soils, biodiversity, ground water) and over-filling nature's waste sinks.[18]

This analysis reveals a hugely important insight. The ecological crisis and justice for poor peoples are inseparable issues. To pillage the ecosphere is to disadvantage those people with the most tenuous hold on the products and services it offers. Climate change and poverty are flip sides of the same problem. We proceed on the understanding of this vital connection.

18. Rees, "Growth through Contraction," 98.

Table 1. Ecological footprints of nations, latest values

Country	footprint, g ha/capita[19]	number of Earths at given footprint[20]	Earth overshoot day[21]
Qatar	10.80	6.6	February 24
Australia	9.31	5.7	March 4
USA	8.22	5.0	March 13
Canada	8.17	5.0	March 13
Kuwait	8.13	5.0	March 13
Austria	6.06	3.7	April 8
New Zealand	5.60	3.4	April 16
Denmark	5.51	3.4	April 16
Germany	5.30	3.3	April 20
France	5.14	3.2	April 23
Japan	5.02	3.1	April 27
China	3.38	2.1	June 22
Brazil	3.11	1.9	July 10
World	**2.75**	**1.69**	**August 4**
Vietnam	1.65	1.01	December 27
Indonesia	1.58	0.97	
India	1.19	0.73	
Nigeria	1.16	0.71	
Ethiopia	1.02	0.63	
Mozambique	0.87	0.53	
Pakistan	0.79	0.48	
Bangladesh	0.72	0.44	
Haiti	0.61	0.37	
Eritrea	0.49	0.30	

19. World Population Review, "Ecological Footprint by Country."

20. Number of Earths required if everyone on Earth consumed at the level of that country (say 5.30 g ha per person for Germany) divided by global biocapacity (world's biocapacity, 1.63 g ha per person) equates to 3.3. We would need at least two additional earths.

21. Date by which annual allocation of biocapacity is used; the time it takes (number of days) to use the annual allocation of Earth production (for 2016, a leap year, 366/no. of Earths).

Extending ecological footprints into other people's territories: trade

Cities have eco-footprints many times larger than the area within their urban boundaries. Many high-income and densely populated countries have eco-footprints several times larger than the area of productive land and sea within their national boundaries.[22] Such cities and countries provide for the needs and wants of their populations by importing ecosystem products from elsewhere (in the case of countries, from other nations). Their ecological footprint is extended into the productive space of other people. For example, to maintain its consumer lifestyle, the UK uses three times as much extraterritorial biocapacity as is contained within its own territorial boundaries.[23]

Rees judges the Kyoto protocol was "well-intentioned but non-effective." The protocol failed because it set targets for GHG emissions *within countries*, with the consequence that GHG-producing industries were simply relocated offshore. The carbon footprint was shifted from wealthy countries into poor ones. This strategy of "carbon leakage" could do nothing to abate CO_2 production.[24]

The benefits of GNP growth accrue mainly to the wealthy.[25] Rich countries live on life-support services imported from other countries. They import land (biophysical capacity) from other nations and impose a disproportionate load on the global commons by dumping their wastes into it.[26] "The enormous purchasing power of the world's richest nations enables them to finance their ecological deficits by extending their ecological footprints deeply into exporting nations."[27] They are effectively land-grabbing. This is twenty-first-century colonialism by stealth.

Rees argues that unlimited economic expansion is fueled by liberalized trade.[28] Unregulated or unfettered trade enables such countries to exceed local carrying capacity, and to deplete [other people's] reserves of natural capital.[29] The effect of globalization is "to expose the world's remain-

22. Rees, "Ecological Footprints," 127–28.

23. Rees, "Avoiding Collapse," 3.

24. Hoekstra and Wiedmann, "Humanity's Unsustainable," 1116–17.

25. Rees, "Ecological Economics Perspective," 25.

26. Rees, "Ecological Economics Perspective," 38; Rees, "Globalization," 263; Rees, "Blot," 838.

27. Rees, "Globalization," 263.

28. Rees, "Globalization," 251.

29. Rees, "Ecological Economics Perspective," 38; Rees, "Avoiding Collapse," 13.

ing pockets of resources to growing numbers of expectant and increasingly affluent consumers," accelerating resource depletion.[30] Ecological havoc is perpetrated out of sight. By this strategy, rich countries are shielded from the direct negative effects of ecosystem degradation.[31]

We maintain our own national parks but convince people in Brazil or New Guinea to destroy their virgin forests in order to provide products for cashed-up consumers. Our demand for palm-oil is destroying orangutan habitat in Indonesia. Our luxury electric cars require cobalt which is being extracted by slave labor in the Democratic Republic of Congo. Rich consumers luxuriating in their electric cars under the guise of "decarbonization" are ravaging distant lands and submitting women and children to inhuman working conditions as they mine our cobalt. But our footprint is largely invisible.[32]

Poor countries are being integrated into the global economy by trade and debt-financed export-led "development." They are coerced into economical structural adjustments (cutbacks in health and education investment) and spend more income on debt servicing than on social services. They accept the destruction of local environments and communities.[33] Those who are impoverished suffer most from ecosystem degradation. In 1998, for the first time, more people fled from weather events and ecological decay than from political upheavals.[34]

Free trade thus accelerates depletion of natural capital and induces nations to create favorable trade imbalances. Competing poor countries decrease prices for commodities and finance the rich by low pay for equally productive work. By the late 1990s, seven dollars flowed to rich countries for every dollar that flowed to poor countries.[35]

Rich countries must reduce their footprints

Are low-income countries locked into poverty because their people are lazy or corrupt? Could they share more of the planetary pie by getting their economic house in order? The answer is, "No!" When the whole pie already

---

30. Rees, "Avoiding collapse," 2–3.
31. Rees, "Ecological Economics Perspective," 39.
32. Sovacool et al., "Decarbonization," 102028.
33. Rees, "Ecological Economics Perspective," 25; Rees, "Globalization," 255.
34. Rees, "Globalization," 256.
35. Rees, "Globalization," 257–58.

has been fully divided up (actually, at the time of writing, 169% of the pie has been claimed), there is nothing left for those who are disadvantaged. If they claimed their fair share of biocapacity, without a corresponding shrinkage of the footprints of rich countries, the ecosphere would be "further jeopardized."[36] To put it bluntly, planet Earth would be scraped bare.

If countries with footprints greater than Earth's biocapacity maintain those footprints, low-income countries cannot *in principle* increase their shares to equitable levels. It follows that economic growth of people in poor countries, just to claim their fair share, will exacerbate strains on the ecosphere *unless there is a corresponding shrinkage of the ecological footprint of rich countries.*[37]

The rich must wake up to the realization "that they might actually have to reduce consumption"—indeed, "the already wealthy must reduce their ecological footprints."[38] New Zealanders would have to reduce their three-Earths lifestyle to a one-Earth lifestyle. That's a two-thirds reduction in consumption and in greenhouse gas emissions. This is a radical decrease in footprint, but it is needed for both ecological sustainability and social justice. The well-off must accept the ethics of "shrink and share" or "contract and converge."[39] In other words, the "environmental footprint of humanity has to reduce toward sustainable levels, and footprints per capita have to converge to similar, more equitable shares."[40]

It follows that if Western people are going to live justly (and share equitably with the people of say, India or sub-Saharan Africa), they must choose a *de-growth* strategy for future planning and living.[41] Indeed, certain societies have used, and are using, economies that do not depend on growth. In reviewing the potential of de-growth economies, Kallis and colleagues write: "Research on past and present alternatives illuminates attributes of low-throughput and steady-state socio-economies, undermining the conviction that there is no alternative to growth."[42]

36. Rees, "Ecological Economics Perspective," 39.
37. Rees, "Ecological Economics Perspective," 39.
38. Rees, "Globalization," 266.
39. Kitzes et al., "Shrink and Share," 467–75.
40. Hoekstra and Wiedmann, "Humanity's Unsustainable," 1116.
41. Rees, "Avoiding Collapse," 8–9.
42. Kallis et al., "Research on Degrowth," 303.

ECOLOGICAL FOOTPRINTS: ANTHROPOLOGY
AND MYTHOLOGY

Rees proposes that the makeup of human beings underlies the ecological crisis and its associated social inequities. Two aspects of our being as *Homo sapiens* predispose us to an ecosphere-wrecking lifestyle. One is our intrinsic nature. We are the product of an unbroken evolutionary history, including 200,000 years as anatomically modern humans. Our biology accounts for our survival as hunter-gatherers, but in the industrial era, it has become maladaptive. The second aspect is to be found in the myths by which we make sense of our world and order our lives. The reigning myth is based on the belief that the human economy can grow in perpetuity, and that our economic activities are independent of ecological reality. This is delusional. In short, ecological overshoot is the predictable outcome of ancient human nature combined with recent cultural nurture.[43] These will be considered in turn.

Human nature

Rees argues that ecological and social unsustainability arise from the very nature of *H. sapiens*. The way humans acquire and share resources "has been shaped, in part, by natural selection."[44] In other words, "a genetic predisposition for unsustainability is encoded in human physiology, social organization, and behavioral ecology."[45]

As biological organisms, humans tend to occupy all available habitats, use all available resources, and diminish the carrying capacity of their habitats. We are *K-strategists*[46]—a species whose population density varies near the carrying capacity (K) of the environment. In new habitats, species such as ours expand exponentially, deplete resources, and undergo population collapse.[47]

As hunter-gatherers, we appropriate what we can get our hands on, locally, and when this is exhausted, simply move on to another patch. This

---

43. Rees, "Growth through Contraction," 100.

44. Rees, "Plague Phase," 2.

45. Rees, "Globalization," 250.

46. Rees, "Plague Phase," 3, 6, 7.

47. Rees, "End Game," 136.

lifestyle identifies us as *patch disturbers*. Such innate (genome-encoded) behavior entails the potential for pathological unsustainability.[48]

Success as a biological species has depended on our ability to maximally exploit energy resources. This is called the *maximum power principle*. But the capacity to efficiently appropriate energy resources reduces the energy that is available to other species. Industrial humanity's success in maximizing its use of energy, especially exosomatic energy from fossil fuels, has supported explosions in both population and in real GDP. Concomitant costs have included resource consumption, rampant waste production, and ecosphere degradation.[49]

Humanity has a record of cycles of heedless growth followed by resource depletion and precipitous collapse. A possible example of this boom-and-bust pattern is furnished by the history of Easter Island, once a verdant tropical paradise. However, over-population and resource depletion caused ecological and societal collapse.[50] Rees asks: "Was it not self-evident that resource depletion in such an obviously finite habitat would lead to disaster?"[51] Humans are feckless, improvident: "collapse seems to be an inevitable stage in the development of human societies."[52] What Rees called the *Easter Island Syndrome* is paradigmatic of humankind's inherent profligacy.[53] Natural selection generally favors individuals who are most adept at satisfying short-term needs ("if we don't claim it, some competitor will").[54] We favor the here-and-now to the exclusion of longer-term imperatives.[55]

Human nature is heedless of consequences. People need to be liberated from its harmful instincts and proclivities. However, most of us

48. Rees, "Ecological Economics Perspective," 35; Rees, "Globalization," 261–62.

49. Rees, "Ecological Economics Perspective," 35–36; Rees, "End Game," 137, 140; Rees, "Plague Phase," 4, 6.

50. Recent evidence queries the mainstream hypothesis of a population catastrophe and suggests that the careful practice of horticulture sustained population resilience. See DiNapoli et al., "Approximate," 3939.

51. Rees, "Globalization," 249.

52. Rees, "Globalization," 250.

53. Rees, "Globalization," 264.

54. John Flenley, a palynologist who studied the history of Easter Island, recounted (at New Zealand's first Creation Care conference, University of Auckland, February 2005) a first-hand instance of the human incapacity to harvest nature responsibly. Flenley suggested to an Easter Islander who had caught a gravid crayfish that if the crayfish was released, it could generate many offspring. But the reply was, "If I do not take this crayfish, someone else will"—the same sentiment reported by Rees, "End Game," 136.

55. Rees, "End Game," 136.

understand neither the nature of our enslavement nor the means of our liberation. "Unless we confront the idea, however dangerous, of our human nature . . . we cannot know what it is we might be alienated from, or what emancipation might mean."[56] We need to grasp that we are in thrall to destructive instincts. As a result of indulging such instincts humans fall short of human potentiality. We could be so much more. We might hope to become truly human as rational but compassionate beings.[57] The alternative is bleak. "*Homo sapiens* will either rise above mere animal instinct and become fully human or wink out ignominiously."[58]

How might we experience emancipation? Rees appeals to certain human capacities and institutions as possible means of remediating our crises in ecological sustainability and moral equity. But he is not confident that these can ameliorate our condition.

First, Rees alludes to an innate *compassion*. He quotes from the *Earth Charter* (2000), that we should "Care for the community of life with understanding, compassion, and love."[59] Compassion is the wellspring from which collaboration might rise: "Sustainability with social justice can be achieved only through an unprecedented level of international cooperation rooted in a sense of compassion for both other peoples and other species."[60] Rees says that "we humans are unlikely to conserve anything for which we do not have love and respect, empathy and compassion."[61]

But then he asks rhetorically, "Would an ostensibly intelligent, forward-thinking, morally conscious, compassionate species continue to defend an economic system that wrecks its planetary home, exacerbates inequality, undermines social cohesion, generates greater net costs than benefits, and ultimately threatens to lead to systemic collapse?"[62] The answer to date is, "Yes." Our native sense of compassion is too weak, too undeveloped, to sustain concerted moral action.

Second, there is our vaunted capacity of *reason*. Beyond our ability to empathize with, and to exercise compassion towards others, we need to give expression to our "capacity to reason logically from available facts

56. David Harvey in Rees, "Globalization," 265.

57. Rees, "Globalization," 265.

58. Rees, "Globalization," 267.

59. Rees, "Globalization," 265.

60. Rees, "Ecological Economics Perspective," 15.

61. Rees, "Globalization," 266.

62. Rees, "Avoiding Collapse," 15.

and data."[63] Humanity must do something about its claims of possessing intelligence, reason, and self-awareness. If people are going to rise above instinct and determinism, they will need to acknowledge their genetic predisposition to, and the socio-cultural mythic roots of, their dysfunctional behavior. The triumph of reason and compassion over scripted determinism would herald a new phase in human cultural evolution.[64]

But reason has ambiguous effects. Humans are both prone to "shortsighted self-delusion" and capable of "high intelligence, reason, introspection, compassion, and even collective action toward a common goal."[65] The capacities of reason and compassion are *possibilities*, aspects of our mentality that do not prevail in the face of challenges to our personal peace and affluence. Rees is realistic about the ability of reason to promote remedial action: "even when convinced of the need for change, people are not wholly rational in dealing with threats to their socio-economic status or political power."[66] Reason is subverted by self-interest. "When humans feel their physical safety or social status is under threat, or they are sorely tempted by some forbidden fruit, the Dr Jekyll of reason may not be able to prevail over the Mr Hyde of emotion or instinct."[67]

Our neurobiology undermines reason. From infancy, exposure to social values lays down synaptic circuits in the brain that filter subsequent inputs. People select information that conforms to their neural presets: "when faced with information that does not agree with their pre-formed neural structures, they deny, discredit, reinterpret, or forget that information."[68] Brains formed in consumerist environments may be inhospitable to ideas that promote sustainable lifestyles.

Human reason is geared to achieve self-preservation, and so is part of the problem. Rees says, "reason alone may not be enough to see us through—after all, it is the calculating rationality of material self-interest that brought the crisis upon us in the first place."[69] Human self-proclaimed reason at the center of the Enlightenment myth is an entirely ambivalent capacity. "*Homo economicus* is an atomistic self-interested utility maximizer

63. Rees, "Avoiding Collapse," 5–6.

64. Rees, "Ecological Economics Perspective," 43; Rees, "Globalization," 249, 267.

65. Rees, "Plague Phase," 8.

66. Rees, "Avoiding Collapse," 7.

67. Rees, "Plague Phase," 6.

68. Rees, "Plague Phase," 8.

69. Rees, "Ecological Economics Perspective," 44.

devoid of family, community, place, and any meaningful relationship with nature; this creature defines 'rational' strictly in terms of maximizing personal consumption."[70]

Cultural myths

All human communities develop and perpetuate myths—stories that make sense of the world and of the community's place in it. Rees observes that modern Western society is as myth-bound as any. Western culture is captivated by the Enlightenment myth of human autonomy. Rees uses "religious" language to describe the prevailing myth. A key *belief* is the *gospel* that growth of human welfare equates to income growth. *Doctrinal authority* for material expansionism is based on neoliberal market economics.[71]

Be warned. The market transforms citizens "into gluttonous single-minded consuming machines." *H. economicus* is morally diminished, unaffected by other people, and has no responsibility to society. Effectively, "greed is good."[72] We are warned that "the modern market model eschews moral and ethical considerations, ignores distributive equity, abolishes the 'common good,' and undermines intangible values such as loyalty to person and place, community, self-reliance, and local cultural mores."[73] Constant repetition of the mantra has conditioned people's thinking. The myth is destroying our social fabric, dissipating the ecosphere, undermining world security.[74]

The myth is *false*. Welfare is not only consumption, but also "a healthy environment, natural beauty, stable communities, safe neighborhoods, economic security, social justice, a sense of belonging."[75] Above a threshold, GDP does not correlate with well-being.[76] Americans are richer but not happier.[77] Rees analyzes several mythical components of our self-destructive mindset.

70. Rees, "Avoiding Collapse," 10.
71. Rees, "Ecological Economics Perspective," 16.
72. Rees, "Ecological Economics Perspective," 18–19; Rees, "Globalization," 251.
73. Rees, "Ecological Economics Perspective," 24; Rees, "Globalization," 255.
74. Rees, "Globalization," 264.
75. Rees, "Globalization," 253.
76. Rees, "Avoiding Collapse," 8–9.
77. Rees, "Globalization," 258.

Myth (a): Growth is disengaged from the ecosphere. Rees states that "the biological predisposition to expand wherever possible is exacerbated by prevailing beliefs and values"—chief amongst which is the myth of sustainable development based on continuous economic growth through globalization and freer trade.[78] Industrialism's "dominant economic paradigm" is based on "global development and poverty alleviation centered on unlimited economic expansion fueled by open markets and more liberalized trade."[79]

To *H. economicus*, the economy is independent of, and not seriously constrained by, the environment. Consequently, according to this paradigm, there is "no fundamental conflict between economic growth and ecological degradation."[80] Neoclassical economics has "abstracted the economic process from nature, viewing it as an independent and 'self-sustaining circular flow between production and consumption,' in which 'complete reversibility is the general rule.'"[81] The economy is regarded as an endlessly circular self-sustaining system of production and consumption—but this perpetual-motion machine is illusory because human activities irreversibly extract resources (energy, materials) from the ecosphere.[82]

The economy is in fact located within, and is a subsystem of, the ecosphere. Both systems require high-quality energy to maintain themselves in a state that is far from thermodynamic equilibrium, and they release low-quality energy (that is, they dissipate useful energy and increase entropy, according to the second law of thermodynamics). The flow of energy is unidirectional. But the ecosphere and the economy dissipate energy in different ways. The ecosphere dissipates solar energy, which is in unlimited supply. The economy dissipates the ecosphere, which is eminently exhaustible.[83]

The assertion of our autonomy is fallacious. Rees has emphasized the discordance between our presumption of independence from nature and our heavy-handed harvest of nature. We are the dominant macroconsumer

78. Rees, "Globalization," 264; Rees, "Growth," 103–4.

79. Rees, "Globalization," 251; Rees, "Blot," 898.

80. Rees, "Ecological Economics Perspective," 17; Rees, "Globalization," 251–52.

81. Quoting Georgescu-Roegen in Rees, "End Game," 135.

82. Rees, "Ecological Economics Perspective," 20–21; Rees, "Globalization," 254; Rees, "End Game," 135; Rees, "Plague Phase," 2.

83. Rees, "Ecological Economics Perspective," 33; Rees, "Globalization," 259; Rees, "Blot," 898; Rees, "Avoiding Collapse," 8; Rees, "End Game," 139, 142; Rees, "Plague Phase," 4–5; Rees, "Growth," 107.

of products in all major terrestrial and marine ecosystems—but claim to have cut ties with nature and consider that the economy floats free from the ecosphere.[84]

Myth (b): Humans can control their lives through technology. The "econo-cultural narrative of perpetual growth and ever-increasing technology" arises from an "anthropocentric utilitarian framework."[85] Rees locates the origins of this myth in the mechanistic vision of Rene Descartes (d. 1650). "This 'scientific materialism' provided the technical foundation of industrial society, and helped entrench a new myth of human dominance over the natural world."[86] Today's technological optimists "believe that modern society has transcended nature, [and] that, sustained by human ingenuity, it is inherently sustainable."[87] The myth assumes that technology has given humans mastery over the natural world.[88] Technology has increased our access to resources and has elevated the short-term carrying capacity of the ecosphere[89]—leaving us poised for an ungainly crash.

Rees argues that technological approaches will not address the problem of unsustainability, because "the world is in thrall to a mythic construct of perpetual material growth abetted by technological progress"—ignoring the fact that the resources upon which growth depends are exhaustible.[90] Indeed, ever-improving fossil-powered technology has facilitated systematic over-exploitation of the world's resources.[91]

Rees provides case-studies of our naïve over-confidence in technologizing life-support processes. *Farmed salmon* has a larger ecological footprint than wild-caught salmon. Every kilogram of product requires feed pellets (production of which requires energy equivalent to 2.4 L diesel fuel) and 4–5 kg of other types of fish (which humans could have consumed directly). Technology replaces a free ecological service: wild salmon are very efficient foragers of relatively unproductive ocean. Factory farming is

84. Rees, "Blot," 898; Rees, "End Game," 137.
85. Rees, "End Game," 142.
86. Rees, "End Game," 135.
87. Rees, "Globalization," 250.
88. Rees, "Globalization," 252.
89. Rees, "Plague Phase," 2–3.
90. Rees, "Plague Phase," 2.
91. Rees, "Growth," 101.

unsustainable. More energy is used in producing the crop than is contained in the product.[92]

Hydroponic tomato cultivation is six- to nine-fold more productive than an equivalent area of traditional agriculture but has an ecological footprint fourteen to twenty times higher. Non-renewables such as gas for heating and fertilizer are substituted for renewable sun and soil.[93]

Renewable sources of energy are offered as solutions to future requirements. Biofuels may reduce carbon footprints but unsustainably increase cropland footprints.[94] Then there is solar and wind power, but the *total* electricity produced by these sources of energy in 2018 (1850 TWh) is equal to the *two-yearly increase* in energy demanded by humanity (1876 TWh).[95] Our appetite for energy is too great for solar and wind power to make a significant contribution.

Technology and liberalized trade are accelerating depletion of nature's warehouse and increasing our indebtedness to nature.[96] Rees criticizes the Paris Accord (2015) for favoring capital-intensive techno-fixes, designed "to serve the capitalist growth economy" (the source of the problem) rather than to achieve reductions in resource use, lifestyle changes, fair income distribution, or population control.[97] Technology and human ingenuity cannot substitute for nature.[98]

Myth (c): Democracy may provide a context for united action. One of the desiderata listed by the *Earth Charter* (2000) is the building of democratic societies.[99] However, the elected leaders of major democracies are bound to the interests of capital and remain blind to humanity's collective predicament. "Growth becomes the default solution to everything from our cumulative debt to nature to chronic poverty. Our propensity for self-delusion may well do us in."[100] Consequently, "Too many current leaders are willing to risk future catastrophe when it will be another's problem."[101]

92. Rees, "Ecological Economics Perspective," 30–31.

93. Rees, "Globalization," 256.

94. Kitzes et al., "Shrink and Share," 3.

95. Rees, "Plague Phase," 5; Rees, "Growth," 105n6.

96. Rees, "Ecological Economics Perspective," 35.

97. Rees, "Plague Phase," 6.

98. Rees, "End Game," 135.

99. In Rees, "Globalization," 265–66.

100. Rees, "Ecological Economics Perspective," 43.

101. Barnard et al., "World Scientists' Warning," 21.

Humanity's unique capacities for collective intelligence, rational analysis, and forward planning for the common good play no major role in the political arena, particularly when they challenge conventional myths, corporate values, and monied elites.[102] And most politicians have never heard of overshoot.[103] Reason plays little role in politics, especially when people's presumption of privilege is challenged.

A generation ago, people might have hoped for the strengthening of democratic process and political transparency. The reality is more sobering. Democracy is in a perilous state in which "corruption and greed (all but sanctioned by contemporary morality) overshadow the public interest."[104] We started this book by acknowledging as Rees does that we live in a post-truth world.[105] An editorial in *Nature* (following the ineffective COP26 meeting of 2021) warned that democracy is in retreat, and this will undermine progress on achieving sustainability.[106]

The Enlightenment has failed. We need "transformation of the fundamental values, beliefs, and assumptions of high-income consumer society. . . . Modern 'man' must consciously deconstruct his failing growth-bound materialist world-view, . . . create a society of material sufficiency in which people find meaning more in relationship."[107] De-growth economics are required, but they are essentially utopian—idealistic dreams that are not likely to be embodied in concrete reality.[108] Kallis and co-authors argue for the adoption of de-growth strategies, but they have an ominous warning. "The end of economic growth without social transformation would lead to destabilization."[109] In other words, human nature and human values must change if human society is to outlast the inevitable curtailment of economic growth by overexploitation of ecological resources.

We are faced with a stark choice. We can demonstrate the very best of our human natures—"cooperative, innovative, wise, and ethical, to learn from mistakes and create better societies—or to go down with both a bang

102. Rees, "Avoiding Collapse," 15.

103. Rees, "Growth," 99.

104. Rees, "Avoiding Collapse," 16.

105. Rees, "Plague Phase," 8.

106. Editorial, "Sustainability," 569–70.

107. Rees, "Ecological Economics Perspective," 15.

108. Kallis et al., "Research," 308.

109. Kallis et al., "Research," 309.

of conflict and a whimper of bickering, entitlement and self-interest."[110] Ecological economists offer penetrating analyses of the science pertaining to climate change and the plight of the victims of consumerism. They are justifiably pessimistic of human capacities to act rightly. Is transformation of human nature and of society a forlorn dream?

ECOLOGICAL FOOTPRINTS: ECOLOGY NEEDS THEOLOGY

Ecological economists have described, in scientific terms, the affliction of the biosphere. They have analyzed, in anthropological terms, the failure of *H. sapiens* to respond adequately. Given our make-up as K-strategist, patch-disturbing, myth-generating animals, our prospects are bleak. We need transformation of our nature, of our worldview, of our beliefs and values and of society itself. Science provides the *indicative*—our perilous situation—in stark terms. But science is unable to provide the *imperative*—the way we should live, and the inner dynamic, the motivated energy, that would enable us to live rightly.

Any talk of *the environment* or *environmentalism* smacks of anthropocentricity. For whose environment is it? The implication is that we are considering the *human* environment. We are preoccupied with *our* needs, *our* security and prosperity, *our* future. We are back to the ambiguity of human reason. An anthropocentric outlook sustains notions of human supremacy, and the very economic expansionism that is ravaging other species and undermining ecological and social stability. "A human-centric worldview is blinding humanity to the consequences of our actions."[111]

The biblical alternative is to adopt a *theo*centric view of the world. A Christian ecological ethic must start with "the knowledge of God as the creator and redeemer of all life."[112] Bill McKibben describes Job 38–39 as the first great piece of nature writing, calling us to cosmic humility, to share God's delight in his creation.[113] Job has been preoccupied with himself, but in this poem, God challenges him with wonderful vistas of creation. As a result, Job's outlook on the world is deconstructed and reordered. Job is reorientated, de-centered; his anthropocentric view and his hubris destroyed.[114]

---

110. Barnard et al., "World Scientists' Warning," 22.

111. Crist, "Reimagining," 1242–44.

112. Northcott, *Ecology and Christian Ethics*, 213.

113. In Bauckham, *Bible and Ecology*, 38, 54.

114. Bauckham, *Bible and Ecology*, 39, 45, 50–51.

In the Psalms, nature points to the glory of the creator, and manifests God's own character (faithfulness, reliability).[115] God rejoices in his works.[116] All creatures, including ourselves, exist to glorify God.[117] This leads us to value planet Earth, not as *our* environment, but as part of *God's* creation.[118] All nature belongs to, and is valued by, God.

> The trees of the LORD are well watered,
> the cedars of Lebanon that he planted . . .
> the earth is full of your creatures.[119]

> "I am God, your God . . . every animal of the forest is mine,
> and the cattle on a thousand hills.
> I know every bird in the mountains,
> and the creatures of the field are mine."[120]

> The earth is the LORD's, and everything in it,
> the world, and all who live in it.[121]

To love nature is vital to caring for it. To love nature's God adds another dimension to that care. When Christians are apathetic regarding (or even hostile to) creation care, they should reassess the reality of their love for God.

The theologian Michael Northcott has stipulated that we must recover an understanding of human beings as divine creation if we are to address the ecological crisis. If we fail to see all creatures, including ourselves, "as gifts of God we are in danger of abusing one another and all creation." To recognize our createdness is to see ourselves and our world as God's gifts. It follows that there is "a deep spiritual connection between our refusal to see ourselves as spiritual beings made in God's image, and our abuse of God's creation." When we stop seeing the world as a creation, we see it simply as something to be engineered for our own use and comfort.[122] To see the world as divine *gift* opens up liberating possibilities. We are beneficiaries of God's grace. To see the world as *a given*, a mere brute fact, leaves us

---

115. Lewis, *Reflections*, 70–71.

116. Ps 104:31; Bauckham, *Bible and Ecology*, 71.

117. Ps 8; 19:1–6; 148; Bauckham, *Bible and Ecology*, 80.

118. Ps 104; Osborn, *Guardians*, 93.

119. Ps 104:16, 24.

120. Ps 50:10–11.

121. Ps 24:1.

122. Ashby et al., "Michael Northcott," 136.

at the mercy of a threatening determinism.[123] Nature—whether human or planetary—just rolls on relentlessly.

But God is not only the *source* of creation. A central understanding of Christian faith is that God has *entered into* and *transformed* creation in the life of Jesus of Nazareth. Gunton has said that "the loving purposes of God for creation . . . are reaffirmed in the incarnation."[124] To Osborn, the incarnation "reminds us that God gives himself to what he has created. And in this self-giving he imparts a genuine, if dependent, existence and a genuine dignity to every creature."[125] God's intimate involvement in the world, is "definitively revealed in the life, death, and resurrection of Jesus Christ, the Incarnate Word."[126] God addresses us in the common matter of the sacraments (water, wine, and bread).[127] Jesus's incarnation and resurrection demonstrate the goodness of matter, motivating us to study it (underlying science, chapter 2) and to cherish it (motivating care of our world whether physical, biotic, or human).

When we think anthropocentrically of the size of the ecological problem, and the infinitesimally tiny contribution that each one of us makes to it, say 10^{-10} (i.e., 1/10,000,000,000) of the whole, paralysis is likely to set in. Our impotence may cause us to become apathetic, or to look for distractions.[128] Why should I forego some luxury when my patterns of consumption make a vanishingly small difference to a planet-wide malaise? Climate change is someone else's problem. We become passive spectators. Inertia rules.

But when we think theocentrically, recognizing nature as creation, we are presented with an imperative to care for God's world and for each other. Moral paralysis is excluded. Even though my own contribution to carbon emissions is infinitesimal, I am accountable to and will be judged by God for every action that affects creation. To serve in the kingdom of God requires obedience in every fleeting and (apparently) insignificant decision. The impact of my footprint is irrelevant. Love for God and his creatures imbues every action with moral significance. The world, as we have noted, whilst not itself divine, is certainly sacred.

123. Osborn, *Guardians*, 134–35.
124. In Northcott, "Ecology and Christian Ethics," 212.
125. Osborn, *Guardians*, 134.
126. Northcott, "Ecology and Christian Ethics," 213.
127. Osborn, *Guardians*, 162.
128. Durrant, *Courting Chaos*, 104.

Nature

Rees noted that compassion has counted for little in our ecological crisis. The *potential* for compassion is genetically encoded, but the *exercise* of compassion is learned from the stories that form us as people—stories, imbibed from infancy, that organize our neural presets. Compassion is nullified by our innate tendency to selfish behavior.[129] Human selfishness and thoughtlessness dominate in behavior underlying the ecological crisis.[130] St. Paul emphasized to his churches the importance of compassion and described the humility of Jesus as the paradigm of self-giving others-orientated living.[131]

And what of *reason*? Northcott agrees with Rees's pessimistic assessment. "Secular reason has trained us no longer to think of ourselves as spiritual beings[;] . . . secular reason has encouraged us to think of the earth as a mechanism which we control through our rational and technological powers. And the latest and most virulently problematic form of secular reason . . . is the ideology of the market as the only way to govern human affairs."[132]

In discussing human nature, Rees alludes to both our reason and to dysfunctional[133] or maladaptive[134] behavior. Reasoned pathological behavior may be given the theological appellation *sin*. God's goodness defines what is good to humans and to all creation, and "the sinful rebellion of the creature against God" disrupts this relational network.[135] *H. economicus* may find the term *sin* demeaning, but recognition of its reality is needed for progress in creation care.

St. Paul recognized that good was foreign to his human nature.[136] The outputs of human nature are ruinous.[137] Extirpation of human nature is necessary[138] and is made possible by Jesus, who came among us with a

---

129. Durrant, *Courting Chaos*, 49.

130. Durrant, *Courting Chaos*, 42.

131. Phil 2:1–11.

132. Ashby, "Michael Northcott," 136.

133. Rees, "Plague Phase," 2, 5; Rees, "Growth," 100, 113.

134. Rees, "Plague Phase, 7, 8; Rees, "Growth," 102.

135. Northcott, "Ecology and Christian Ethics," 220.

136. Rom 7:18, 25.

137. Gal 5:17, 19–21; Rom 8:5–8.

138. Gal 5:24; Eph 4:22.

nature like our own—but not polluted with sin.[139] St. John wrote of God's self-disclosure in Jesus, "the Word became flesh"—where *flesh* is human nature in its vulnerability, weakness, and its commonality with the rest of creation. Flesh is "human nature made out of the dust of the earth, utterly dependent on all the physical conditions of life on this planet."[140] Jesus's humanity was physically continuous with ours but morally discontinuous with ours; truly *H. sapiens*, but innocent of the exploitative urges of *H. economicus*.

The gospel teaches that we need the infusion of Christ's nature as an ongoing,[141] albeit fragile,[142] process, otherwise described as the creative activity of God's Spirit.[143] We grow to participate in the divine nature through worship and reading of scripture, to caring for one another and to working for God's kingdom on Earth. Those who participate in the trinitarian divine nature learn to foster the relationships that comprise the communities of creatures.[144]

The gospel announces an alternative to our innate ecosphere-despoiling nature. But it is often hard to perceive concrete effects of that gospel in the habits of people who claim to adhere to it. There is also the issue of the myths by which we live. We are very vulnerable to the seductive myths of our consumerist age.

Myths and idols

Rees critiqued the myths and activities defining *H. economicus*. Northcott concurs on point after point. Wealth enables people to extend their ecological footprints beyond the territories in which they live.[145] Big business extracts surplus value from African lands,[146] and exports its GHG emissions offshore.[147] Industrialism excludes peasant farmers and tribal peoples

139. Rom 8:3.

140. Bauckham, "Jesus," 223–24.

141. Eph 4:23–24; Col 3:10; 2 Pet 1:4.

142. Gal 4:19.

143. Gal 5:16; Rom 8:4, 9, 13.

144. Northcott, *Moral Climate*, 183–84.

145. Northcott, *Moral Climate*, 151–52.

146. Northcott, *Moral Climate*, 50.

147. Northcott, *Moral Climate*, 58.

from their traditional habitats.[148] Climate change is most damaging to the poorest people,[149] and is life-threatening to the most vulnerable.[150]

Northcott affirms the goal of contraction and convergence but laments the reality as expansion and divergence.[151] The wealthy are enmeshed in a cult of consumerism.[152] Energy-hungry systems of industrialism corrode moral character.[153] Conventional economic theory asserts that economic growth (as defined by GDP) increases human welfare "regardless of the ecological destruction and waste involved."[154] Market models are "covert valuing devices in which human lives and ecosystems are traded against economic growth."[155] Neoliberalism perpetuates the lie that unrestrained economic growth leads to progress and peace.[156]

Rees and Northcott diagnose the same malaise and seek alternatives to the economistic myth. Here, the biblical narrative provides special illumination. To Northcott, our worship "is at the heart of our ecological crisis. It is precisely the modern devotion to the cult of consumerism which is driving the horrific global scale of environmental destruction." Northcott argues that our uncontrolled appetite for consumer goods is a spiritual disease; that Western civilization shows "devotion to that which is not God"; and that this misplaced devotion is *idolatry*, the "worship of created things in the place of God."[157] Northcott concludes: "the modern substitution of the idols of consumerism for the worship of God [is] the fundamental theological and spiritual challenge posed by the environmental crisis."[158] An idol is something made by human hands, which people worship, and to which they give their "soul force" in service.[159]

148. Northcott, "Ecology and Christian Ethics," 222; *Moral Climate*, 41, 169.

149. Northcott, *Moral Climate*, 29.

150. Northcott, *Moral Climate*, 56.

151. Northcott, *Moral Climate*, 132–33; see also Houghton, "Why Care?" 248.

152. Northcott, "Spirit of Environmentalism," 168, 174.

153. Northcott, *Moral Climate*, 33.

154. Northcott, *Moral Climate*, 143.

155. Northcott, *Moral Climate*, 148.

156. Northcott, *Moral Climate*, 39.

157. Northcott, "Spirit," 168.

158. Northcott, "Spirit," 174.

159. Ashby, "Michael Northcott," 135.

Idols destroy their devotees. "When humans devote themselves to things . . . they devote themselves to lies,"[160] destroy their societies and sacrifice their children. "A society that sets monetary measures of expanding wealth such as the rate of increase of GDP at its heart is a society that has dethroned God, . . . an idolatrous society that will sacrifice people and species and the earth system itself to the gods of mammon."[161] *Things, lies, wealth,* and *GDP* are listed as contemporary gods. Anthropocentric outlooks are inherently idolatrous. It follows that "systematic engagement with modern idolatry and the lies that the idols sustain" affect the way we consume fossil fuels.[162] The "devotion to the gods of secular reason, technological power, and monetary accumulation" associated with industrial capitalism comes to fruition in greenhouse gas accumulation.[163]

Jesus revealed the kingdom of God, providing the vision to live rightly on earth. God provides the resources of creation for all members of the community of God's creatures, both human and non-human (birds, wildflowers).[164] But God provides for people's *needs*, not for their obsessive anxieties over ever-increasing standards of living.[165]

Jesus called people to reject the pursuit of affluence and to follow him; to choose between serving money and serving God.[166] This idea was mocked by the avaricious Pharisees. Jesus asked, "Does a person gain anything if he wins the whole world but loses his life?"[167] This could be taken as oblique critique of the hegemonic ambitions of the ruling class. Jesus taught people that they should not store up riches for themselves on earth.[168] He charged them to sell all their belongings and give the money to the poor.[169] A wealthy Jewish leader slunk away dejected because he could not act on Jesus's injunction. With oriental hyperbole, Jesus said that it was easier for

160. Northcott, "Sustaining Ethical Life," 227.

161. Northcott, "Sustaining Ethical Life," 230–31.

162. Northcott, "Sustaining Ethical Life," 228.

163. Northcott, *Moral Climate,* 14.

164. Matt 6:25–34.

165. Bauckham, *Bible and Ecology,* 74–75.

166. Matt 6:24/Luke 16:13–14.

167. Mark 8:36/Matt 16:26/Luke 9:25.

168. Matt 6:19–21/Luke 12:32–34.

169. Luke 12:33.

a camel to pass though the eye of needle than for a rich man to enter the kingdom of God.[170]

Jesus warned that those who lived in affluence faced disaster: "you have had your easy life."[171] He told parables about the folly of pursuing wealth. A rich farmer accumulated wealth for his retirement but died before he could enjoy any of it.[172] The crux of his folly was his preoccupation with material wealth (Fig. 6, top). Jesus's application is pertinent to an ecological and social ethic. "Watch out and guard yourselves from every kind of greed; because a person's true life is not made up of the things he owns, no matter how rich he may be."[173] The farmer's misdirected priorities typify all "those who pile up riches for themselves and are not rich in God's sight."[174] True wisdom is to be concerned above all else with God's kingdom.[175] To Northcott, the story of the rich fool is "about the wickedness of greed and lust for power, and the willingness to store up an excess of God's creation in such a way that it actually becomes a source of death rather than life."[176]

170. Mark 10:17–31/Matt 19:16–30/Luke 18:22–30.

171. Luke 6:24–26.

172. Luke 12:13–21.

173. Luke 12:15.

174. Luke 12:21.

175. Luke 12:31/Matt 6:33.

176. Ashby, "Michael Northcott," 137.

13-14 Setting: inheritance dispute

15 teaching: life is not possessions
    16 possessions gained: crops
       17 soliloquy: "what shall I do?"
        18 plan: "build bigger barns"
      19 soliloquy: "take life easy"
    20 possession lost: life
  21 teaching: rich for self, not God

2-4 endure—be perfect, complete, lacking nothing
    5 lack wisdom? God gives generously
      6 doubt—lifeless wave
       7-8 undecided, receive nothing
        9 poor, glad, God lifts up [spiritually]
        10-11 rich, glad, God lowers [materially]
      12 remain faithful, receive life
    13-15 evil desire, sin—death
  16-17 deceived? God's good gifts, perfect presents
18 God gives being, first place among all creatures

1 believing in Jesus Christ—don't treat people by outward appearance
    2-3a rich given undue honour
      3b-4 poor dishonoured
       5 poor chosen to be rich in faith
       poor chosen to possess the Kingdom
      6a poor dishonoured
    6b-7 rich oppress, speak evil
8-9 obeying the Law of the Kingdom—don't treat people by outward appearance

1 you rich people: miseries are coming to you
    2-3a your riches witness against you
      3b you have piled up riches
       4 you have not paid your workers
       their cries are heard by God
      5a your life is full of luxury and pleasure
    5b you are fattened for slaughter
6 you rich people: you have condemned the innocent

Fig. 6. Poverty and riches in the teaching of Jesus and James
Rhetorical analyses (from top to bottom) of Jesus's parable of the rich fool (Luke 12:13–21,
adapted from Bailey, *Jesus*, 298), and discussions of poverty and wealth in Jas 1:2–18; 2:1–9;
and 5:1–6. The paragraphs from James also form chiastic structures (author's analysis). In
all cases, hope for the impoverished or warnings for the wealthy comprise the central focus.

The parable of the rich man and the beggar Lazarus[177] describes the
reversal of their fortunes in the hereafter. The rich man took up the beggar's

177. Luke 16:19–31.

standard cry, "Have pity on me!"[178] This was a scandalous inversion of worth as held by many first-century Jews, for whom worldly wealth evinced God's approval. Jesus repudiated the formula that equates wealth with divine blessing, poverty with sinfulness. Among other things, the parable is a call to economic equity.[179]

The letter of James may well have come from the brother of Jesus and leader of the Jerusalem church.[180] The community to which James wrote was scattered (by persecution?). James was himself murdered at the instigation of the high priest in AD 62.[181] As Jesus had done before him, James criticized the abuses of the rich. He echoed Jesus[182] by asserting that the poor should rejoice because God raised them (spiritually) to a new dignity, hope, and calling. The rich should be glad when they were brought down (materially) to a new space where they could learn humility and dependence on God (Fig. 6, second from top).[183] The poor were rich in faith and responded to the invitation to possess God's kingdom. The rich were oppressors. People with genuine faith clothed and fed the needy (Fig. 6, third from top).[184] The rich withheld payment from their workers. Their ill-gotten luxuries evinced their guilt and ripened them for punishment (Fig. 6, bottom).[185]

Jesus's care for deprived and vulnerable people subverted and still subverts prevailing economic values. His call for justice in place of acquisitive living supplants consumerism. To adopt Jesus's paradigm is to gain inner motivation to live sustainably and justly.

---

178. Bailey, *Jesus*, 388 (ελέησόν με, cf. Luke 16:24 with 18:38).

179. Bailey, *Jesus*, 395–96.

180. Evans, *From Jesus to the Church*, 22; cautiously, Wright and Bird, *New Testament in Its World*, 734–35.

181. Evans, *From Jesus to the Church*, 107–9.

182. Matt 5:3; Luke 4:16–21; 6:20.

183. Jas 1:9–10; Durrant (*Courting Chaos*, 109–13) draws similar points from the object lesson of the baskets of figs (Jer 24). The "good figs" (the exiles languishing in Babylon) may have been motivated into more honest theological reflection (p. 111). The "bad figs" (the fortunate people still residing in the comfort of Jerusalem) were callously indifferent to the needs of the exiles and are analogous to the wealthy trusting in their economy and technology. Paradoxically, it is the former (poor) people who are blessed.

184. Jas 2:5–7, 14–17.

185. Jas 5:2–6.

Obedience to God, ecological health

Northcott criticizes modern secular ethics as "a project of creative construction." In other words, secular ethicists think they are at liberty to construct their own version of "the good." Nature is understood to be "autonomous uncaused mechanism," so that "the order of nature has no prior moral significance" and (according to philosopher Peter Singer) ethics is not part of the structure of the universe. This materialistic view is congenial to "the modern economistic and technocentric construction of nature as resource bank for industrial, chemical, and organic re-ordering for human purposes."[186]

Northcott rejects the idea that what is good is a product of the human mind. The belief that humans construct "the good" sunders moral from scientific reasoning and explains why modern thought disconnects the flourishing of humans from the flourishing of the ecosphere.[187] Faith in God engendered the confidence that there is an objective reality (truth) about the physical world, and so promoted scientific thinking (chapter 2). The idea that God is guarantor of truth also establishes the objectivity of morality, including that pertaining to creation.

Faith in a creator God who is good establishes that goodness and justice are embedded in creation. The ancient Israelites recognized the moral character of God and creation.[188] A moral law is written into the created order.[189] In particular, justice is a universal, a divine attribute set into the structure of God's world.[190] As Northcott says, the "righteousness and justice that are intrinsic to the being of God are also writ large in the material and moral framework of the creation."[191]

Idolatry and injustice inflict damage on[192] and oppress[193] humans, other biota, and physical nature. The objectivity of righteousness underlies and unites the quest for ecological sustainability and social justice. Human actions that reflect God's justice affirm and promote the wholeness

---

186. Northcott, "Ecology and Christian Ethics," 216.

187. Northcott, "Ecology and Christian Ethics," 217.

188. Northcott, *Moral Climate*, 71.

189. Northcott, "Spirit," 171.

190. Northcott, *Moral Climate*, 12, 64–65, 160.

191. Northcott, "Ecology and Christian Ethics," 221–22.

192. Northcott, *Moral Climate*, 164.

193. Northcott, "Spirit," 169.

of creation. Right worship leads to fertility of the land and the harmony of creation.[194] Righteousness and ecological health are connected in the covenant:

> See, I set before you today life and prosperity, death and destruction. For I command you today to love the LORD your God, to walk in obedience to him, and to keep his commands, decrees and laws; then you will live and increase, and the LORD your God will bless you in the land you are entering to possess.[195]

Loving obedience to God is coupled to fertility of the land. It is not that a servile people can coax favors from a miserly God. Rather, obedience to God's covenant establishes the conditions in which the ecology of the land best flourishes. Nor should God's judgment be understood as divine pique, but as the natural consequence of people's disobedience. As Bauckham says, "frequently in the Bible, language of divine judgement describes the way acts have consequences in this world. Disruption of the created order of things causes further disruption that rebounds on the perpetrators."[196] To Durrant, we may "understand God's wrath as the handing over of people to suffer the consequences of their sinful actions."[197]

Jeremiah may be the first ecological prophet in literary and religious history. He argued that Israel had neglected divine justice and righteousness, and consequently had upset the divinely given order of creation.[198]

> These people do not say to themselves,
> "Let us fear the LORD our God,
>   who gives autumn and spring rains in season,
>   who assures us of the regular weeks of harvest."
> Your wrongdoings have kept these away;
>   your sins have deprived you of good.[199]

Neglect of God's laws, including the Sabbath law, led to the idolatrous worship of objects, generated excessive ecological demands, and issued in

---

194. Northcott, "Spirit," 170; Osborn concurs: according to the wisdom tradition, disharmony in the moral sphere has serious consequences for the natural (Isa 24:1–13; Hos 4:1–3); *Guardians*, 94.

195. Deut 30:15–16; NIV.

196. Bauckham, *Bible and Ecology*, 100–101 (comma added for clarity).

197. Durrant, *Courting Chaos*, 16, 28.

198. Northcott, "Spirit," 170; *Moral Climate*, 12–13.

199. Jer 5:23–25, NIV.

Israel's downfall.[200] Human behavior has repercussions for the very structure of the planet. Human evil sabotaged God's protective measures: a controlled sea, ordered climate, and regular seasons.[201]

> Why has the land been ruined and laid waste like a desert? The LORD said, "It is because they have forsaken my law, . . . they have not obeyed me, . . . they have followed the Baals."[202]

Jeremiah repeatedly connected Israel's infidelity and the land's infertility. With the spread of idolatry, the land became a desert, formless and empty (like the primeval chaos of Gen 1:2).[203] With wickedness, the land became parched.[204] Bauckham states, "Human evil has ecological consequences," and quotes Brueggemann: "Covenantal Israel held the staggering notion that human conduct matters for the well-being of creation."[205] Northcott said that "greed or the will to power, arrogance or aggression, and not infrequently injustice and oppression in human society have gone hand in hand with ecological destruction."[206]

Isaiah also stressed how justice is embedded in the world. Spencer and White state of Isa 40–65 that, "whether we like it or not, there is an irreducible and far-reaching moral element in the issue of sustainable living. The created order is inherently moral and, if we wish to sustain it, we cannot ignore our moral obligations."[207] Isaiah connected exclusion of the poor from the land and the land's loss of fertility.[208]

> Woe to you who add house to house and join field to field
> till no space is left and you live alone in the land.
> The LORD Almighty has declared in my hearing:
> "Surely the great houses will become desolate,
> the fine mansions left without occupants."
> A ten-acre vineyard will produce only [twenty-two liters] of wine,
> [160 kg] of seed only [sixteen kg] of grain.[209]

---

200. Northcott, *Moral Climate*, 11, 13.

201. Durrant, *Courting Chaos*, 8.

202. Jer 9:10–14.

203. Jer 4:23–28.

204. Jer 12:4.

205. Bauckham, *Bible and Ecology*, 94.

206. In Bauckham, *Bible and Ecology*, 95.

207. Spencer and White, *Christianity*, 108.

208. Northcott, "Ecology and Christian Ethics," 220–21; also, Isa 30:21–23; 32:15–16.

209. Isa 5:8–10, NIV.

The earth dries up and withers,
the world languishes and withers,
the heavens languish with the earth.
The earth is defiled by its people;
   they have disobeyed the laws,
violated the statues
   and broken the everlasting covenant.[210]

In contrast, God's redemption of his chastened people restores the land's fertility.[211] Or, as Spencer and White say, "environmental regeneration is not to be understood in isolation from social redemption."[212] Ecology morphs into eschatology.

Holiness is connected with sustainability through cause-and-effect logic. God's covenant with the people contained provisions that protected smallholders and their land. The weekly Sabbath was a reminder that the land was God's, a gift and not a commodity; work was holy and time sanctified. Farmers and animals rested. In Sabbath years, the land rested, the economy was restrained, poor people and wild animals could help themselves to the untended fields. In Jubilee years, the fields lay fallow, land alienated by debt was returned to families, and debt slaves released.[213]

This equilibrium was upset when the worship of God was neglected in favor of idol worship. The Sabbaths were forgotten. Israel's militaristic rulers became preoccupied with power, Israel's elites with wealth.

Trade in surplus products and tax considerations benefitted city merchants and forced the peasants into cultivating cash crops, for which the soil was unsuitable and about which the farmers knew nothing. Cash-cropping disrupted ecologically harmonious practices (crop rotation, fallowing, seasonal interaction between pastoral and agricultural activities). Perennial grasses were replaced with cereals, promoting salinization. Unsuitable land which erodes easily was cultivated. Deforestation led to droughts, flash floods, and soil erosion. Denuded land absorbed more sunlight. Reduced rainfall promoted desertification.[214]

---

210. Isa 24:4–5.

211. Isa 35:1–7; 44:1–5.

212. Spencer and White, *Christianity*, 104.

213. Lev 25:8–55, Spencer and White, *Christianity*, 121–26, 137–43.

214. As still happens. Deforestation in Brazil contributes to the increasing intensity and frequency of droughts, both locally (less moisture is transferred from the Amazon rainforests to the south-central agricultural region) and globally. Getirana et al., "Brazil," 218–20.

Anything that disrupted production had catastrophic consequences. Farmers had to procure food on credit, pawn their children as debt slaves, or work as laborers. Before long, they lost their ancestral land. A large group of landless paupers arose. They worked for large estate owners who lived in dissolute luxury in the cities. The people and land had become impoverished and enslaved.[215]

Israel's plight illuminates ours. The crisis Jeremiah faced and his analysis of it speak to the ecological consequences we are reaping from having broken our covenant with God.[216] God's justice is written into creation, even if human wisdom cannot see it.

The basis of democracy

Is Rees unduly pessimistic about the state of democracy? Not according to Northcott, who perceives democracy as being undermined by materialism.[217] Political paralysis prevails because of the neoliberal dogma "that only continued and unfettered growth in the consumption of goods and services in a borderless international 'free' trade regime can advance human well-being."[218] But maximized economic growth, as routinely promised by politicians, can only exacerbate the problem.[219]

> The leaders of the rich nations are elected on the basis of a collective lie . . . that they will make the lives of voters better, and their communities fairer and more prosperous, by allowing economic corporations to continue to rip through the ecosystems of the earth and the social fabric of human communities. . . . Politicians will not tell the truth about climate change and ecological collapse.[220]

215. From Northcott, "Ecology and Christian Ethics," 220; Northcott, *Moral Climate*, 4, 8, 10–11; Olivier, "Historical," 156–57. Dispossession of smallholders continues in Africa. "Modernisation" of farming (low-interest loans, new crop varieties, artificial fertilizers, absorption into global supply chains) leads to debt, takeover of land by businessmen, and migration of former smallholders to city slums. Park and Vercillo, "African Agriculture."

216. Durrant, *Courting Chaos*, 173.

217. Alluding to de Tocqueville, in Northcott, "Sustaining Ethical Life," 234.

218. Northcott, "Sustaining Ethical Life," 236.

219. Durrant, *Courting Chaos*, 174, 183–84.

220. Northcott, *Moral Climate*, 35.

Authentic democracy and righteous economic systems are insepa-rable. Theologian John De Gruchy argues that true democracy must mean a "democracy of wealth." Uncontrolled capitalism hinders democratic trans-formation.[221] "If the free-market system is to help rather than hinder the flourishing of genuine democracy, then it has to become less the servant of greed and more the servant of social justice."[222] De Gruchy continues, "As long as the free market treats labour, land, and money as commodi-ties separated from the lives and needs of people, it impedes democratiza-tion"—because economic advantages accrue only to elites.[223]

To talk of democracy begs the question—on what "myth" or story is democracy based? Democracy first appeared in Christian history,[224] and this suggests that the biblical narrative should disclose the moral basis and source of its vitality. According to popular opinion, democracy came from classical Greece. But the Greek "tyranny of citizens" entertained no concept of human rights,[225] and indeed was a foreshadowing of apartheid.[226] De Gruchy has written: "The democratic *vision* has its origins, not so much in ancient Athens, the symbolic birthplace of the democratic *system*, as in the message of the ancient prophets of Israel, and especially in their messianic hope for a society in which the reign of God's *shalom* [wholeness] would become a reality."[227] To Theo Hobson, "the Bible has a passion for social justice that pagan thought lacks."[228] The Bible taught an ethical universal-ism that associated God's will with social justice, and it condemned cultic traditions that neglected this.[229]

The prophetic tradition arose from the story of Israel's liberation from slavery in Egypt. The prophets proclaimed God's concern for the poor and oppressed. They sought to "bring about a society in which all people are equally respected as bearers of God's image."[230] The king should not be above his fellows. Israel was called to emulate God's care for the poor,

---

221. De Gruchy, *Christianity and Democracy*, 24.

222. De Gruchy, *Christianity and Democracy*, 25.

223. De Gruchy, *Christianity and Democracy*, 26.

224. Northcross, *Moral Climate*, 282–83.

225. De Gruchy, *Christianity and Democracy*, 16.

226. Knight, *I AM*, 41.

227. De Gruchy, *Christianity and Democracy*, 7.

228. Hobson, *God Created Humanism*, 23.

229. Hobson, *God Created Humanism*, 36–37.

230. De Gruchy, *Christianity and Democracy*, 11.

for widows and orphans, and for the oppressed; to practice social justice (*tzedakah*); to minimize social inequities (achieved in part by the Jubilee year); and to cherish relationships between God, the people, and creation, so upholding *shalom*.[231] Israel failed to implement these requirements, but the prophetic texts "provided the basis for an ongoing radical critique of social domination and its legitimating ideologies."[232]

Jesus extended the prophetic tradition. He proclaimed God's righteousness as the basis for social renewal: good news for the poor, release for prisoners, healing for the blind, freedom for the oppressed, the year of God's favor, and the renewal of society and of creation.[233] He disregarded social, gender, or cultic barriers. His brand of righteousness, *tzedakah*,[234] challenged the Sadducean plutocracy.[235] Jesus's parables taught that all people should be treated equally (the good Samaritan) and that practical morality is more important than cultic practice (the sheep and the goats).[236] God's new order rejected political systems that arose through violence. Rather, it came through the suffering of its Savior, who rejected worldly power and wealth and died as an outcast.[237]

The early church was an egalitarian community.[238] Baptism signified membership in God's new humanity, and "a radical rejection of all divisive social distinctions." St. Paul's abolition of barriers between "Jew and gentile, slave and free, male and female"[239] was deeply subversive. The church called itself the *ekklesia* (Greek for the assembly of citizens), a universal community drawn from every segment of society, a social plurality, the new humanity belonging to a new world order.[240] Spencer has said that "the Church was inclusive and universal in a way that nothing else was in the

---

231. De Gruchy, *Christianity and Democracy*, 42–44.

232. De Gruchy, *Christianity and Democracy*, 45.

233. Luke 4:18–21, cf. Isa 61:1–2.

234. Matt 6:33.

235. De Gruchy, *Christianity and Democracy*, 46–48.

236. Hobson, *God Created Humanism*, 35.

237. Hobson, *God Created Humanism*, 37–38.

238. Acts 2:43–47.

239. Gal 3:28; 1 Cor 12:13; Col 3:11.

240. De Gruchy, *Christianity and Democracy*, 49–51; Hurtado, *Destroyer*, 55–56, 93–94.

ancient world, its sacraments emphasizing the individuality and equality of all."[241]

In an accident of history, the emperor Constantine polluted this vision by conferring imperial patronage upon the church. But counter-cultural reform movements, in which class distinctions were obliterated and resources shared, emerged repeatedly.[242] When the biblical vision was repudiated by state-backed (supposedly) Christian institutions, it inspired and was carried forward by secular movements.[243] For example, in the eighteenth century, secular writers such as Voltaire denounced the evils associated with the church by appealing to standards that "were distinctively, peculiarly Christian."[244] The virtues upon which democracy rests—such as the equal value of all humans—originated with the prophets of Israel and with Jesus. As biblical influence declines, the foundations of democracy will be eroded progressively.[245] Democracies of government and of economies may not be there to help as ecosphere collapse looms closer.

Repentance

Christian faith contributes an important and distinctive concept to creation care because it possesses the language of *repentance*[246]—a word that translates the Greek *metanoia*, a change (*meta-*) of mind (*-noia*). To *repent* is to turn away from evil practices, such as (in our current context) misdirected worship and its concomitant creation-abuse. We must acknowledge that we are responsible for the "structures of sin" as a first step in redemption (or salvation) from them.[247]

---

241. Spencer, *Evolution*, 14.

242. De Gruchy, *Christianity and Democracy*, 59–60.

243. Hobson, *God Created Humanism*, chs. 3 and 4.

244. Holland, *Dominion*, 394–95. To the (largely) Deist founding fathers of the United States, the principles of equality, inalienable rights, and liberty were "self-evident," but they are in fact far from self-evident. Such principles were rooted in the Bible (*Dominion*, 400–401).

245. Hart, *Atheist Delusions*, 237–38; Hobson, *God Created Humanism*, 139, 142–48; Spencer, *Evolution*, 71, 77, 79; Wright, *Surprised by Scripture*, 195.

246. I thank ethicist and philosopher Dr. Murray Sheard of A Rocha NZ for this insight.

247. Northcott, *Moral Climate*, 183.

Repentance was central to the preaching of John the Baptist,[248] of Jesus,[249] and of the apostles. Repentance was required of Jews, Samaritans, and pagans[250]—and Christians, including affluent Laodiceans,[251] leaving no room for complacency or triumphalism. Christians have been widely apathetic regarding climate change and economic justice. It is all too easy to sustain aspirations to ever-increasing affluence that are not compatible with the gospel of Jesus. A presumption to live in luxury, even as others who equally bear God's image are mired in penury, is incompatible with the ethos of the kingdom of God.[252]

Repentance requires sorrow (articulated as lament) for wrongs that have been done, alongside a commitment to completely redirect one's priorities and behavior—to undergo a radical change of mind and heart.[253] Contemporary church worship has emphasized celebration over lament; but when faced with intractable evil, such as the plunder of God's Earth, it needs to express lament.[254]

> I will weep and wail for the mountains
> and take up a lament for the wilderness grasslands.
> They are desolate and untraveled,
> and the lowing of cattle is not heard.
> The birds have all fled and the animals are gone.
> The LORD said, "It is because they have forsaken my law."[255]

Durrant suggests that lament challenges us to face reality, to wake up to sin and its effects on the land, to accept responsibility, and to act. It underlies a change from apathy to engagement with God and to a new valuation of nature.[256]

Humans identify salvation with economic development, material wealth, and technological control.[257] Repentance is a necessary condition of the salvation effected by Jesus, which involves release from people's

248. Mark 1:4/Matt 3:2/Luke 3:3.

249. Mark 1:14/Matt 4:17; Luke 13:5.

250. Acts 2:38; 3:19; 8:22; 17:30.

251. Rev 2:5, 16, 23; 3:19.

252. Jas 2:15–16; 1 John 3:17–18.

253. Northcott, "Sustaining Ethical Life," 226–27.

254. Durrant, *Courting Chaos*, 99.

255. Jer 9:10, 13.

256. Durrant, *Courting Chaos*, 101–5.

257. Northcott, *Moral Climate*, 58.

sinful rebellion, and liberation of the whole creation.[258] Reconciliation with God and reconciliation with creation are natural partners[259] and require fidelity to the spiritual foundations upon which the ecosphere and society are based.[260]

But given the failure of humanity to engage rightly with the rest of creation, is hope contingent upon repentance and reconciliation any more realistic than Rees's wistful appeal to reason, compassion, or democracy? The biblical precedents are not encouraging. Amos and Hosea could not deflect Israel from the path that led to annihilation by Assyria. Jeremiah failed to restrain Judah from its headlong rush to destruction by Babylon. Jesus was unable to call Israel back from its descent into cataclysmic conflict with Rome. The affluent church provides little evidence that it will be renewed *en masse*, or that it will be converted to pursuing the ethics of Jesus, as taught for example in his Sermon on the Mount and demonstrated in his sacrifice on the cross.

The paradigm of suffering servanthood shown by the prophets and uniquely by Jesus has enriched the world beyond measure. Spencer and White have said that "the wholeness [*shalom*] of all creation is achieved by an act of unmatched self-sacrifice, by way of the cross"—counter-intuitive though it may seem.[261] Jesus's sacrificial death provides salvation for all who submit to his way of being human. God calls people to emulate Jesus amidst our descent into socio-political and environmental chaos. Sacrifice enabling sustainable living will provide purpose and fulfilment and engender joy: "in spite of the size of the problem and the moral demands it places upon us, the conclusion is a cause of celebration."[262] Repentance involves both sacrifice (taking up our cross)[263] and joy (taking Jesus's yoke).[264]

Jesus's teaching haunts the complacent. Movements of renewal have repeatedly appeared as alternatives to the god of affluence. When the fourth-century church was absorbed into the machinery of empire, the desert fathers exiled themselves, in order "to recover the soul they were in danger of losing" to the collusive relationship with power and wealth.

258. Northcott, "Ecology and Christian Ethics," 220.

259. Bauckham, *Bible and Ecology*, 178.

260. Northcott, *Moral Climate*, 15.

261. Alluding to Isa 53:5; Spencer and White, *Christianity*, 116.

262. Spencer and White, *Christianity*, 115.

263. Mark 8:34/Matt 16:24/Luke 9:23.

264. Matt 11:29–30; Spencer and White, *Christianity*, 117.

Subsequently, St. Benedict (d. 547) led the ascetic monastic "quest to be true to the radical call of the gospel."[265] God may yet work in ways that cannot be anticipated.

Hope to live by

Can we hope for peace in our time? Climate change and overshoot are problems of catastrophic dimensions. They arise from human selfishness and egregious abuses of the biosphere. Human beings seem to be incapable of corrective action when their choices clearly have them careering to disaster, to chaos. As Rees and other scientists emphasize, our prospects are dire.

But the story of God's action in the world offers hope. This does not deny that humanity will experience severe dislocation. But it provides a way and motivation to live for others, a sense of meaning in what would otherwise be meaningless, of purpose in situations that would otherwise engender nihilistic despair, and an inspiring vision of what God will yet create in the face of threatening chaos. According to Konig, a theme of scripture is that God's creative work controls chaos, gains victory over chaos, and protects the creatures from chaos.[266] Chaos is understood in this context as disorder and confusion, and it is represented metaphorically in the Hebrew Scriptures by darkness, the sea, or the mythical sea monsters.

But more than gaining victory over chaos, God creates out of chaos. New things are made from disasters. Out of chaos God purposes to bring peace, wholeness, joy and living fellowship.[267] From the chaos of the Babylonian exile, God brought salvation to the broken people of Israel. The dry bones scattered across the Mesopotamian valley would be resurrected as a reinvigorated people of God.[268] From the chaos of Jesus's crucifixion came resurrection.[269] In the chaos of the world, God's purpose is to bring people into his *shalom* in union with Jesus.[270] The biblical "good" is the "creation of what is wholly new out of chaos, the realm of pain, sorrow, earthquakes,

---

265. Ashby, "Michael Northcott," 137. Hart shares the same pessimism and hope for renewal movements as in the past, *Atheist Delusions*, 238–41.

266. Konig, *New and Greater Things*, 17, 45, 47, 51, 72, 76–78, 122, 145–56.

267. Knight, *I AM*, 36.

268. Knight, *I AM*, 39.

269. Durrant, *Courting Chaos*, 88.

270. Knight, *I AM*, 52.

famines, [plus ecological overshoot and climate change] and—most important of all—the sin and rebellion that is characteristic of the human mind and heart."[271]

We have considered how the story of God's redeeming action in history enabled the pioneers of science to see time as linear, not meaninglessly cyclic (chapter 2); and that turning points in this history were so surprising that they had to represent *a reality discovered*, not *dogmas invented* (chapter 5). Christian faith is based (counter-intuitively!) on two facts of history that epitomized the chaos of destruction—and that were transformed into the splendor of new life. These events were the annihilation of Jerusalem (587 BC) and the crucifixion of Jesus (AD 30 or 33),[272] a chaotic abyss from which resurrection emerged.[273]

But chaos is not merely raw material for God's action. According to Knight, God uses evil or chaos as his *servant* (the italics are mine). God creates by *employing* chaos, by using chaos as an *instrument* of God's purpose. God constantly creates good *by means* of chaos, or *with the help of* an evil situation. God *employs* the chaos (meaninglessness) of human life to create what is new and complete.[274]

Such historical precedents engender confidence that the chaos of ecological destruction is not the terminus of human history. The world will be transformed by God into new creation. Social chaos, the loss of cherished human institutions (science, democracy), and our suffering planet will be transformed by God into right worship, compassion and justice, and the harmonious relationships that characterize *shalom*. The loss of venerable (but misguided) traditions may empty Christians of their egos and accreted heresies and so allow them to pour out their souls in sacrificial service modelled on Christ's.[275] In the chaos of absolute self-emptying, the person who follows Jesus can be reborn to joyful service.

271. Knight, *I AM*, 22.

272. Knight, *I AM*, 89.

273. Durrant, *Courting Chaos*, 87.

274. Knight, *I AM*, 21, 22, 26, 32, 44.

275. Knight, *I AM*, 69–70. Knight elaborates on this principle. Isaiah became aware of his total inadequacy (he had to be reduced to nothing) before he could be God's spokesman. Isaiah discovered that "the holy seed will be the stump in the land"—the destruction of Israel (the "stump") is "a new beginning for God's people" (Isa 6:13, NIV cf. GNT). The blood of the martyrs is the seed of the church (Tertullian). An end to humanity's futile religions, philosophies, and social reconstructions must precede new life (Professor Joseph Hromadha, reflecting on the destruction of Czechoslovakia in 1945)

Jeremiah is renowned as a prophet of doom, but he expressed hope in God's purposes: "the LORD says . . . the whole land will be ruined, though I will not destroy it completely."[276] Jeremiah could retain a sense of hopeful anticipation, not because the situation provided reasons for a facile optimism, but because of God's goodness, which would triumph over human evil. "That hopefulness is based on who God is. It is not so much a hope *for* as a hope *in*, specifically a hope *in* God or *in* his law."[277] Isaiah urged Israel to have faith that the creator God is trustworthy, despite the trauma of exile. We should exercise that same faith, despite the magnitude of the task ahead of us.[278]

We live and work in the anticipation of God's new creation, the consummation of the created order.[279] In this goal, the creative and redemptive plans of God come together, as aspects of the one overarching purpose, to be achieved by Christ and the Spirit.[280]

> This plan, which God will complete when the time is right, is to bring all creation together, everything in heaven and on earth, with Christ as head.[281]

The prospect of a new creation pervades the writings of Jesus's first followers.[282] The sense of confident anticipation of creation's transformation issues from the resurrection of Jesus, the prototypical instance, the founding event. Northcott describes how the bodily resurrection of Jesus is of the utmost significance for the physical world. Jesus's resurrection is the basis of the resurrection also of humankind in union with him, and necessarily therefore of all creation with him.[283] To Durrant, the redemption of our physical bodies is linked to redemption of our physical planet.[284]

---

in Knight, *I AM*, 64–65.

276. Jer 4:27.

277. Spencer and White, *Christianity*, 112.

278. Spencer and White, *Christianity*, 113.

279. Osborn, *Guardians*, 97, 98, 100.

280. Northcott, "Ecology and Christian Ethics," 213; Jesus both creates and redeems; Col 1:15–20; Heb 1:1–3; John 1:1–18.

281. Eph 1:9–10.

282. 1 Cor 15:25–28; Rom 8:21; Col 1:20; 2 Pet 3:13; Rev 21–22.

283. Paraphrasing Oliver O'Donovan, in Northcott, "Ecology and Christian Ethics," 214–15.

284. Durrant, *Courting Chaos*, 39; citing Rom 8:18–23.

Created beings will be taken into the life of the triune God. The goal of the cosmos is deification, *theosis*.[285] This does not mean that creation becomes divine, but that the Spirit or life of God is infused into it. God will dwell in a consummated creation.[286] Ecosphere-wrecking creatures have been regenerated to become the home (*oikos*—the Greek root of *eco*logy or *eco*nomy) of the triune creator God. Human beings have plundered and despoiled their God-given *oikos* but will themselves be the *oikos* of the holy God.

> God's Spirit lives (or dwells, *oikei*, οικει) in you![287]

> God himself has said, "I will make my home [dwell, *enoikeso*, ενοικησω] with my people."[288]

> I pray that Christ will make his home [may dwell, *katoikesai*, κατοικησαι] in your hearts through faith.[289]

> If the Spirit of God, who raised Christ from death, lives [dwells, *oikei*, οικει] in you, then he who raised Christ from death will also give life to your mortal bodies by the presence [indwelling, *enoikountos*, ενοικουντος] of his Spirit in you.[290]

There is a future for our *oikos*, the ecosphere. It will possess the *shalom* that God has always intended to endow upon it.[291] Is this a selfish other-worldly fantasy that frees us from any responsibility to care for victims of climate change and environmental refugees—whether those victims are non-human biota or humans? Absolutely not—the conviction that God is intimately involved in the world's history provides the utmost motivation for Jesus's followers to live energetically and sacrificially to bring God's wholeness to every victim of human greed.

---

285. Osborn, *Guardians*, 127.

286. Wright, *Paul and the Faithfulness of God*, 1021–22.

287. 1 Cor 3:16 (GNT).

288. 2 Cor 6:16.

289. Eph 3:17.

290. Rom 8:(9), 11.

291. Northcott, "Ecology and Christian Ethics," 215.

BIBLIOGRAPHY

Aitken, John T., et al. *The Influence of Christians in Medicine*. London: Christian Medical Fellowship, 1984.

Alexander, Denis. *Are We Slaves to Our Genes?* Cambridge: Cambridge University Press, 2020.

———. *Rebuilding the Matrix: Science and Faith in the 21st Century*. Oxford: Lion, 2001.

Ashby, Roland. "Michael Northcott: Our Devotion to Idols Is Killing the Planet." In *A Reckless God?* edited by Roland Ashby et al., 133–37. Reservoir Victoria, Australia: ISCAST Nexus, 2018.

Baguley, Bruce C., et al. "DNA-Binding Anticancer Drugs: One Target, Two Actions." *Molecules* 26 (2021) article 552.

Bailey, Kenneth E. *Jesus through Middle Eastern Eyes*. Downers Grove, IL: IVP, 2008.

Barnard, Phoebe, et al. "World Scientists' Warnings into Action: Local to Global." *Science Progress* 104 (2021) 368504211056290.

Bauckham, Richard. *Bible and Ecology*. London: Darton, Longman and Todd, 2010.

———. "Jesus, God and Nature in the Gospels." In *Creation in Crisis*, edited by Robert S. White, 209–24. London: SPCK, 2009.

Bero, Lisa. "Stamp Out Fake Clinical Data by Working Together." *Nature* 601 (2022) 167.

Bimson, John J. "Considering a 'Cosmic Fall.'" *Science and Christian Belief* 18 (2006) 63–81.

Blomqvist, Linus, et al. "Does the Shoe Fit? Real Versus Imagined Ecological Footprints." *PLoS Biology* 11 (2013) e1001700.

Boyd, Robert, et al. "The Cultural Niche: Why Social Learning Is Essential for Human Adaptation." *Proceedings of the National Academy of Sciences of the USA* 108 Suppl 2 (2011) 10918–25.

Boyd, Robert L. F. "Reason, Revelation and Faith." In *Christianity in a Mechanistic Universe and Other Essays*, edited by Donald M. MacKay, 109–25. London: Inter-Varsity Fellowship, 1965.

Briggs, Andrew, Hans Halvorson, and Andrew Steane. *It Keeps Me Seeking*. Oxford: Oxford University Press, 2018.

Brooke, John H. *Science and Religion: Some Historical Perspectives*. Cambridge: Cambridge University Press, 1991.

Cahill, Thomas. *How the Irish Saved Civilization*. London: Hodder and Stoughton, 1995.

Chapman, Allan. *Slaying the Dragons*. Oxford: Lion Hudson, 2013.

Chawla, Dalmeet Singh. "A Single 'Paper Mill' Appears to have Churned Out 400 Papers, Sleuths Find." doi:10.1126/science.abb4930.

Copan, Paul, and Douglas Jacoby. *Origins: The Ancient Impact and Modern Implications of Genesis 1–11*. Nashville: Morgan James, 2019.

Coulson, Charles A. *Science and Christian Belief*. London: Fontana, 1958.

Crist, Eileen. "Reimagining the Human." *Science* 362 (2018) 1242–44.

Crow, James M. "The Māori Meeting House That's Also a Research Lab." *Nature* 598 (2021) 228.

De Gruchy, John W. *Christianity and Democracy*. Cambridge: Cambridge University Press, 1995.

Diaz, Sandra, et al. "Pervasive Human-Driven Decline of Life on Earth Points to the Need for Transformative Change." *Science* 366 (2019) eaax3100.

DiNapoli, Robert J., et al. "Approximate Bayesian Computation of Radiocarbon and Paleoenvironmental Record Shows Population Resilience on Rapa Nui (Easter Island)." *Nature Communications* 12 (2021) article 3939.

Dixon, Thomas. *Science and Religion: A Very Short Introduction*. Oxford: Oxford University Press, 2008.

D'Mello, Stacey A. "The Role of Endonuclease G in the Action of the Antitumour Drug Paclitaxel." MSc diss., University of Auckland, 2011.

Durrant, Kevin. *Courting Chaos: Navigating the Ecological Crisis with the Help of Jeremiah*. Eugene, OR: Wipf and Stock, 2021.

Editorial. "COVID Scientists in the Public Eye Need Protection from Threats." *Nature* 598 (2021) 236.

———. "Replicating Scientific Results Is Tough—But Essential." *Nature* 600 (2021) 359–60.

———. "Sustainability at the Crossroads." *Nature* 600 (2021) 569–70.

Efron, Noah. "Myth 9. That Christianity Gave Birth to Modern Science." In *Galileo Goes to Jail and Other Myths about Science and Religion*, edited by Ronald L. Numbers, 79–89. Cambridge, MA: Harvard University Press, 2009.

Else, Holly. "China's Clampdown on Fake-Paper Factories Picks Up Speed." *Nature* 598 (2021) 19–20.

———. "'Tortured Phrases' Give Away Fabricated Research Papers." *Nature* 596 (2021) 328–29.

Else, Holly, and Richard Van Noorden. "The Fight against Fake-Paper Factories That Churn Out Sham Science." *Nature* 591 (2021) 516–19.

Evans, Craig A. *From Jesus to the Church*. Louisville, KY: Westminster John Knox, 2014.

Ferngren, Gary B. *Medicine and Religion: A Historical Introduction*. Baltimore: John Hopkins University Press, 2014.

Finlay, Graeme J. *Evolution and Eschatology: Genetic Science and the Goodness of God*. Eugene, OR: Cascade, 2021.

———. *The Gospel According to Dawkins*. London: Austin Macauley, 2017.

———. *Human Evolution: Genes, Genealogies and Phylogenies*. Cambridge: Cambridge University Press, 2013.

Finlay, Graeme J., and Bruce C. Baguley. "Selectivity of N-[2-(Dimethylamino)-Ethylacridine-4-Carboxamide towards Lewis Lung Carcinoma and Human Tumour Cell Lines *In Vitro*." *European Journal of Cancer and Clinical Oncology* 25 (1989) 271–77.

Fletcher, Michael-Shawn, et al. "Indigenous Knowledge and the Shackles of Wilderness." *Proceedings of the National Academy of Sciences of the USA* 118 (2021) e2022218118.

Getirana, Augusto, et al. "Brazil Is in Water Crisis—It Needs a Drought Plan." *Nature* 600 (2021) 218–20.

Gingerich, Owen. *God's Planet*. Cambridge: Harvard University Press, 2014.

———. *God's Universe*. Cambridge: Harvard University Press, 2006.

———. "What Does Physics Tell Us about God?" *Science and Christian Belief* 13 (2001) 98.

Goodman, David, and Colin A. Russell, eds. *The Rise of Scientific Europe 1500–1800*. Milton Keynes, UK: The Open University, 1991.

Hannam, James. *God's Philosophers: How the Medieval World Laid the Foundations of Modern Science*. London: Icon, 2009.

Harrison, Peter. *The Bible, Protestantism, and the Rise of Natural Science*. Cambridge: Cambridge University Press, 1998.

———. "Christianity: The Womb of Western Science." In *A Reckless God?* edited by Roland Ashby et al., 17–24. Reservoir Victoria, Australia: ISCAST Nexus, 2018.

———. "Religion, the Royal Society, and the Rise of Science." *Theology and Science* 6 (2008) 255–71.

———. "Science, Religion, and Modernity." https://www.giffordlectures.org/lectures/science-religion-and-modernity.

———. *The Territories of Science and Religion*. Chicago: University of Chicago Press, 2015.

Hart, David B. *Atheist Delusions*. New Haven, CT: Yale University Press, 2009.

———. *The Experience of God*. New Haven, CT: Yale University Press, 2013.

Hellstrom, Per M. "This Year's Nobel Prize to Gastroenterology: Robin Warren and Barry Marshal Awarded for Their Discovery of *Helicobacter Pylori* as Pathogen in the Gastrointestinal Tract." *World Journal of Gastroenterology* 12 (2006) 3126–27.

Helm, Paul. "Why Be Objective?" In *Objective Knowledge*, edited by Paul Helm, 31–40. Leicester, UK: IVP, 1987.

Hobson, Theo. *God Created Secular Humanism*. London: SPCK, 2017.

Hoekstra, Arjen Y., and Thomas O. Wiedmann. "Humanity's Unsustainable Environmental Footprint." *Science* 344 (2014) 1114–17.

Holland, Thomas. *Dominion: How the Christian Revolution Remade the World*. New York: Basic, 2019.

Holt, Rush. "Democracy's Plight." *Science* 363 (2019) 433.

Hooykaas, Reijer. *Religion and the Rise of Modern Science*. Edinburgh: Scottish Academic Press, 1972.

Hotez, Peter J. "Anti-Science Kills: From Soviet Embrace of Pseudoscience to Accelerated Attacks on US Biomedicine." *PLoS Biology* 19 (2021) e3001068.

Houghton, John. *The Search for God: Can Science Help?* Oxford: Lion, 1995.

———. "Why Care for the Environment?" In *Has Science Killed God?* edited by Denis Alexander, 238–50. London: SPCK, 2019.

Huff, Toby E. *Intellectual Curiosity and the Scientific Revolution*. Cambridge: Cambridge University Press, 2011.

Hurtado, Larry E. *Destroyer of the Gods*. Waco, TX: Baylor University Press, 2016.

Hutchings, David, and Tom McLeish. *Let There Be Science: Why God Loves Science and Science Needs God*. Oxford: Lion Hudson, 2017.

Instone-Brewer, David. *The Jesus Scandals*. Oxford: Monarch, 2012.

Jaki, Stanley L. *Science and Creation*. Edinburgh: Scottish Academic Press, 1986.

Judge, Edwin. "Religion of the Secularists." *Journal of Religious History* 38 (2014) 307–19.

Kaiser, Christopher. *Creation and the History of Science*. London: Marshall Pickering, 1991.

Kallis, Giorgos, et al. "Research on Degrowth." *Annual Review of Environment and Resources* 43 (2018) 291–316.

Keane, Phoebe "How the Oil Industry Made Us Doubt Climate Change." BBC, 20 Sept 2020. https://www.bbc.com/news/stories-53640382.

Kim, Ji Eun, et al. "Heterogeneity of Expression of Epithelial-Mesenchymal Transition Markers in Melanocytes and Melanoma Cell Lines." *Frontiers in Genetics* 4 (2013) 97.

Kittelson, James M. *Luther the Reformer*. Leicester, UK: IVP, 1989.

Kitzes, Justin, et al. "Shrink and Share: Humanity's Present and Future Ecological Footprint." *Philosophical Transactions of the Royal Society Series B* 363 (2008) 467–75.

Knight, George A. F. *I AM: This Is My Name*. Grand Rapids: Eerdmans, 1983.

Konig, Adrio. *New and Greater Things*. Pretoria: UNISA, 1988.

Kumar, Prasanna, and Frederick A. Murphy. "Francis Peyton Rous." *Emerging Infectious Diseases* 19 (2013) 660–63.

Lewis, C. S. *Miracles*. London: Bles, 1947.

———. *The Problem of Pain*. Glasgow: Fontana, 1957.

———. *Reflections on the Psalms*. Glasgow: Collins and Sons, 1961.

Lewis, Geraint F., and Luke A. Barnes. *A Fortunate Universe*. Cambridge: Cambridge University Press, 2016.

Lindberg, David C. "Science in the Early Church." In *God and Nature*, edited by David C. Lindberg and Ronald L. Numbers, 19–48. Chicago: Chicago University Press, 1986.

Livingstone, David N. *Darwin's Forgotten Defenders*. Grand Rapids: Eerdmans, 1987.

———. "Myth 17: That Huxley Defeated Wilberforce in Their Debate over Evolution and Religion." In *Galileo Goes to Jail and Other Myths about Science and Religion*, edited by Ronald L. Numbers, 152–60. Cambridge, MA: Harvard University Press, 2009.

Lucas, Ernest. *Science and the New Age Challenge*. Leicester, UK: IVP, 1996.

MacKay, Donald M. *The Clockwork Image*. London: IVP, 1974.

———. "Objectivity as a Christian Value." In *Objective Knowledge*, edited by Paul Helm, 15–27. Leicester, UK: IVP, 1987.

———. *Science and the Quest for Meaning*. Grand Rapids: Eerdmans, 1982.

McCarthy, James. "Climate Science and Its Distortion and Denial by the Misinformation Industry." In *Creation in Crisis*, edited by Robert S. White, 34–52. London: SPCK, 2009.

McGrath, Alister. *Dawkins' God: Genes, Memes, and the Meaning of Life*. Oxford: Blackwell, 2005.

McLeish, Tom. *Faith and Wisdom in Science*. Oxford: Oxford University Press, 2014.

———. "Thinking Differently about Science and Religion." *Physics Today* 71 (2018) 10–12.

———. "What Is Science and What Is It For?" ISCAST/NZCIS Lecture, 27 May 2021, https://www.youtube.com/watch?v=HqTPF_7Mq10.

McLeish, Tom C. B., et al. "A Medieval Multiverse." *Nature* 507 (2014) 161–63.

McMullin, Ernan. "The Galileo Affair." In *Has Science Killed God?* edited by Denis Alexander, 51–64. London: SPCK, 2019.

Meilaender, Gilbert. *Bioethics: A Primer for Christians*. Carlisle, UK: Paternoster, 1996.

Nogrady, Bianca. "Scientists under Attack." *Nature* 598 (2021) 250–53.

Nola, Robert. "Courage Needed to Expose 'Post-Truth' Fallacy." *NZ Herald*, 26 Dec 2016. https://www.nzherald.co.nz/opinion/news/article.cfm?c_id=466&objectid=11772969.

Northcott, Michael S. "Ecology and Christian Ethics." In *The Cambridge Companion to Christian Ethics*, edited by Robin Gill, 209–27. Cambridge: Cambridge University Press, 2001.

———. *A Moral Climate: The Ethics of Global Warming*. Maryknoll, NY: Orbis, 2007.

———. "The Spirit of Environmentalism." In *The Care of Creation*, edited by R. J. Berry, 167–74. Leicester, UK: IVP, 2000.

———. "Sustaining Ethical Life in the Anthropocene." In *Creation in Crisis: Christian Perspectives on Sustainability*, edited by Robert S. White, 225–40. London: SPCK, 2009.

Olivier, Hannes. "Historical-Geographical Setting of the Old Testament." In *Plutocrats and Paupers: Wealth and Poverty in the Old Testament*, edited by Hendrik L. Bosman et al., 131–58. Pretoria: J. L. van Schaik, 1991.

Oreskes, Naomi, and Eric M. Conway. *Merchants of Doubt*. London: Bloomsbury, 2010.

Osborn, Lawrence. *Guardians of Creation: Nature in Theology and the Christian Life*. Leicester, UK: Apollos, 1993.

Osler, Margaret J. "Myth 10. That the Scientific Revolution Liberated Science from Religion." In *Galileo Goes to Jail and Other Myths about Science and Religion*, edited by Ronald L. Numbers, 90–98. Cambridge: Harvard University Press, 2009.

Park, Alex, and Siera Vercillo. "African Agriculture without African Farmers." 9 Oct 2021. https://www.aljazeera.com/opinions/2021/10/9/african-agriculture-without-its-farmers.

Polkinghorne, John. *Beyond Science*. Cambridge: Cambridge University Press, 1996.

———. *One World*. London: SPCK, 1986.

———. *Quarks, Chaos and Christianity*. London: Triangle, 1994.

———. *Reason and Reality*. London: SPCK, 1991.

———. *Science and Christian Belief*. London: SPCK, 1994.

———. *Science and Creation*. London: SPCK, 1988.

———. "The Science and Religion Debate: An Introduction." In *Has Science Killed God?* edited by Denis Alexander, 3–13. London: SPCK, 2019.

Portin, Petter. "The Birth and Development of the DNA Theory of Inheritance: Sixty Years since the Discovery of the Structure of DNA." *Journal of Genetics* 93 (2014) 293–302.

Prance, Ghillian. *The Earth Under Threat*. Glasgow: Wild Goose, 1996.

Proctor, Robert N. "The History of the Discovery of the Cigarette-Lung Cancer Link: Evidentiary Traditions, Corporate Denial, Global Toll." *Tobacco Control* 21 (2012) 87–91.

Rees, William E. "Avoiding Collapse: An Agenda for Sustainable Degrowth and Relocalizing the Economy." Climate Justice Project. Vancouver, BC: Canadian Centre for Policy Alternatives-BC and University of BC, 2014. https://www.policyalternatives.ca/sites/default/files/uploads/publications/BC%20Office/2014/06/ccpa-bc_AvoidingCollapse_Rees.pdf.

———. "A Blot on the Land." *Nature* 421 (2003) 898.

———. "Eco-Footprint Analysis: Merits and Brickbats." *Ecological Economics* 32 (2000) 371–74.

———. "Ecological Economics for Humanity's Plague Phase." *Ecological Economics* 169 (2020) 106519.

———. "An Ecological Economics Perspective on Sustainability and Prospects for Ending Poverty." *Population and Environment* 24 (2002) 15–46.

———. "Ecological Footprints and Appropriate Carrying Capacity: What Urban Economics Leaves Out." *Environment and Urbanization* 4 (1992) 121–30.

———. "End Game: The Economy as Eco-Catastrophe and What Needs to Change." *Real-World Economics Review* 87 (2019) 132–48.

———. "Globalization and Sustainability: Conflict or Convergence?" *Bulletin of Science, Technology and Society* 22 (2002) 249–68.

———. "Growth through Contraction: Conceiving an Eco-Economy." *Real-World Economics Review* 96 (2021) 98–118.

Rees, William E., and Mathis Wackernagel. "The Shoe Fits but the Footprint Is Larger Than Earth." *PLoS Biology* 11 (2013) 1001701.

Rhodes, Frank H. T. "Christianity in a Mechanistic Universe." In *Christianity in a Mechanistic Universe and Other Essays*, edited by Donald M. MacKay, 11–48. London: Inter-Varsity Fellowship, 1965.

Ross, John. "New Zealand Academics Investigated over Maori Knowledge Letter." *Times Higher Education*, 6 Dec 2021. https://www.timeshighereducation.com/news/new-zealand-academics-investigated-over-maori-knowledge-letter.

Rudwick, Martin J. S. *Earth's Deep History*. Chicago: University of Chicago Press, 2014.

Russell, Colin A. *Cross-Currents: Interactions between Science and Faith*. Leicester, UK: IVP, 1985.

Shank, Michael H. "Myth 2. That the Medieval Christian Church Suppressed the Growth of Science." In *Galileo Goes to Jail and Other Myths about Science and Religion*, edited by Ronald L. Numbers, 19–27. Cambridge: Harvard University Press, 2009.

Shen, Helen. "Seeing Double." *Nature* 581 (2020) 132–36.

Sidik, Saima M. "Weaving Indigenous Knowledge into the Scientific Method." *Nature* 601 (2022) 285–87.

Sovacool, Benjamin K., et al. "The Decarbonization Divide: Contextualizing Landscapes of Low-Carbon Exploitation and Toxicity in Africa." *Global Environmental Change* 60 (2020) 102028.

Spencer, Nick. *The Evolution of the West*. Louisville, KY: Westminster John Knox, 2018.

Spencer, Nick and Robert White. *Christianity, Climate Change and Sustainable Living*. London: SPCK, 2007.

Stang, Adreas, et al. "A Twenty-First Century Perspective on Concepts of Modern Epidemiology in Ignaz Philipp Semmelweis' Work on Puerperal Sepsis." *European Journal of Epidemiology* 37 (2022) 437–445.

Steane, Andrew. *Faithful to Science*. Oxford: Oxford University Press, 2014.

Supran, Geoffrey. "Fueling Their Own Climate Narrative." *Science* 374 (2021) 702A-B.

Thorson, Walter R. "The Spiritual Dimensions of Science." In *Horizons of Science*, edited by Carl F. H. Henry, 217–57. New York: Harper and Row, 1977.

———. "Scientific Objectivity and the Listening Attitude." In *Objective Knowledge*, edited by Paul Helm, 61–83. London: IVP, 1987.

Trigg, Roger. *Beyond Matter*. Conshohocken, PA: Templeton, 2015.

———. "Does Science Need Religion?" In *Has Science Killed God?* edited by Denis Alexander, 14–23. London: SPCK, 2019.

Turner, Harold. "Recasting Establishment History: The Roots of Science." In *Science and Christianity*, edited by L. Robert B. Mann, 149–76. Auckland: University of Auckland Centre for Continuing Education, 2001.

———. "Religion: Impediment or Saviour of Science?" *Science and Education* 5 (1996) 155–64.

———. *The Roots of Science*. Auckland: DeepSight Trust, 1998.

Van Noorden, Richard. "Hundreds of Gibberish Papers Still Lurk in the Scientific Literature." *Nature* 594 (2021) 160–61.

———. "Journals Adopt AI to Spot Duplicated Images in Manuscripts." *Nature* 601 (2022) 14–15.

Wackernagel, Mathis, and Bert Beyers. *Ecological Footprint: Managing Our Biocapacity Budget*. Gabriola Island, BC: New Society, 2019.

Wagner, Roger, and Andrew Briggs. *The Penultimate Curiosity: How Science Swims in the Slipstream of Ultimate Questions*. Oxford: Oxford University Press, 2016.

Weiss, Robin A., and Peter K. Vogt. "100 Years of Rous Sarcoma Virus." *Journal of Experimental Medicine* 208 (2011) 2351–55.

Wenham, Gordon J. *Genesis 1–15*. WBC 1A. Waco, TX: Word, 1987.

Whitehead, Andrew L., and Samuel L. Perry. "How Culture Wars Delay Herd Immunity: Christian Nationalism and Anti-Vaccine Attitudes." *Socius* 6 (2020) 1–12.

Wilkinson, David. *God, the Big Bang and Stephen Hawking*. Tunbridge Wells, UK: Monarch, 1993.

Willyard, Cassandra. "New Human Gene Tally Reignites Debate." *Nature* 558 (2018) 354–55.

Woods, Thomas E. *How the Catholic Church Built Western Civilization*. Washington, DC: Regnery, 2005.

World Population Review. "Ecological Footprint by Country 2022." https://worldpopulationreview.com/country-rankings/ecological-footprint-by-country.

Worthing, Mark W. *God, Creation, and Contemporary Physics*. Minneapolis: Augsburg Fortress, 1996.

———. *Unlikely Allies: Monotheism and the Rise of Science*. Eugene, OR: Wipf and Stock, 2019.

Wright, N. T. *How God Became King*. London: SPCK, 2012.

———. *Jesus and the Victory of God*. London: SPCK, 1996.

———. *The New Testament and the People of God*. London: SPCK, 1992.

———. *Paul and the Faithfulness of God*. London: SPCK, 2013.

———. *The Resurrection of the Son of God*. London: SPCK, 2003.

———. *Surprised by Scripture: Engaging with Contemporary Issues*. London: SPCK, 2014.

Wright, N. T. and Michael F. Bird. *The New Testament in its World*. London: SPCK, 2019.

Young, Toby. "Why Punish a Scientist for Defending Science?" *Spectator*, 4 Dec 2021. https://www.spectator.co.uk/article/why-punish-a-scientist-for-defending-science-.

INDEX